**Congressional
Research Service**
Informing the legislative debate since 1914 _____

The Defense Production Act of 1950: History, Authorities, and Reauthorization

Jared T. Brown
Analyst in Emergency Management and Homeland Security Policy

Daniel H. Else
Specialist in National Defense

July 30, 2014

Congressional Research Service

7-5700

www.crs.gov

R43118

CRS REPORT
Prepared for Members and
Committees of Congress _____

Summary

The Defense Production Act (DPA) of 1950 (P.L. 81-774, 50 U.S.C. Appx §2061 et seq.), as amended, confers upon the President a broad set of authorities to influence domestic industry in the interest of national defense. The authorities can be used across the federal government to shape the domestic industrial base so that, when called upon, it is capable of providing essential materials and goods needed for the national defense.

Though initially passed in response to the Korean War, the DPA is historically based on the War Powers Acts of World War II. Gradually, Congress has expanded the term *national defense,* as defined in the DPA, so that it now includes activities related to homeland security and domestic emergency management. The scope of DPA authorities extends beyond shaping U.S. military preparedness and capabilities, as the authorities may also be used to enhance and support domestic preparedness, response, and recovery from natural hazards, terrorist attacks, and other national emergencies.

The current authorities of the DPA include, but are not limited to:

- **Title I: Priorities and Allocations**, which allows the President to require persons (including businesses and corporations) to prioritize and accept contracts for materials and services as necessary to promote the national defense.

- **Title III: Expansion of Productive Capacity and Supply**, which allows the President to incentivize the domestic industrial base to expand the production and supply of critical materials and goods. Authorized incentives include loans, loan guarantees, direct purchases and purchase commitments, and the authority to procure and install equipment in private industrial facilities.

- **Title VII: General Provisions**, which includes key definitions for the DPA and several distinct authorities, including the authority to establish voluntary agreements with private industry; the authority to block proposed or pending foreign corporate mergers, acquisitions, or takeovers that threaten national security; and the authority to employ persons of outstanding experience and ability and to establish a volunteer pool of industry executives who could be called to government service in the interest of the national defense.

The authorities of the DPA are generally afforded to the President in statute. The President, in turn, has delegated these authorities to department and agency heads in Executive Order 13603, *National Defense Resource Preparedness*, issued in 2012. While the authorities are most frequently used by, and commonly associated with, the Department of Defense, they can be, and have been, used by numerous other executive departments and agencies. The DPA lies within the jurisdiction of the House Committee on Financial Services and the Senate Committee on Banking, Housing, and Urban Affairs.

Nearly all DPA authorities will terminate on September 30, 2014, though a few, such as the Exon-Florio Amendment (which established government review of the acquisition of U.S. companies by foreigners) and anti-trust protections for certain voluntary industry agreements, have been made permanent. Since 1950, the DPA has been reauthorized over 50 times, though significant authorities were terminated from the original law in 1953. Congress last reauthorized the DPA in 2009 (P.L. 111-67, the Defense Production Act Reauthorization of 2009). This reauthorization amended some of the current DPA authorities and extended the termination of the act by five years.

H.R. 4809, as passed by the House under suspension of the rules on July 29, 2014, would reauthorize the DPA until September 30, 2019. Among other changes, H.R. 4809 would reform the purpose and structure of the Defense Production Act Committee (DPAC), emphasize an existing rulemaking requirement for Title I priorities and allocations authority, and restore several limitations on the President's Title III authorities that were removed in the Defense Production Act Reauthorization of 2009. The bill would also authorize appropriations for the carrying out of the provisions and purposes of this act in the amount of $133 million every fiscal year beginning in FY2015.

Contents

Tables

Appendixes

Contacts

Introduction

The Defense Production Act of 1950, as amended (DPA),[1] provides the President a broad set of authorities to ensure that domestic industry can meet national defense requirements. In the DPA, Congress has found that "the security of the United States is dependent on the ability of the domestic industrial base to supply materials and services for the national defense and to prepare for and respond to military conflicts, natural or man-caused disasters, or acts of terrorism within the United States."[2] Through the DPA, the President can, among other activities, prioritize contracts for goods and services, and offer incentives within the domestic market to enhance the production and supply of critical materials and technologies when necessary for national defense. Since 1950, the DPA has been reauthorized over 50 times by Congress, most recently in 2009.[3] The majority of DPA authorities will expire on September 30, 2014, unless reauthorized.

This report examines some of the extensive history of the DPA, focusing primarily on its creation and most recent legislative reauthorization. This report also discusses the foremost active authorities of the DPA. Nevertheless, this report is not intended to evaluate all authorities of the DPA comprehensively. In discussing the major authorities of the DPA, this report explains how those authorities may have changed as a result of the most recent reauthorization of the law (P.L. 111-67, the Defense Production Act Reauthorization of 2009, henceforth referred to as "Reauthorization of 2009").[4] This report also identifies relevant delegations of the President's DPA authorities made in Executive Order (E.O.) 13603, *National Defense Resources Preparedness*.[5] Finally, this report provides a brief overview of issues relevant to Congress and tracks legislation in the 113th Congress to reauthorize the DPA. H.R. 4809 was reported out of the Committee on Financial Services in the House of Representatives on June 11, 2014. If enacted, H.R. 4809 would reauthorize the DPA for five years and would reform other provisions, as discussed later in the report. The report also discusses congressional considerations for expanding, restricting, or otherwise modifying the authorities provided by the DPA, either in conjunction with or separate from a reauthorization.

History of the DPA

Origin

The DPA was inspired by the First and Second War Powers Acts of 1941 and 1942, which gave the executive branch broad authority to regulate industry during World War II.[6] Much of this

---

[1] 50 U.S.C. Appx. §§2061 *et seq.*

[2] 50 U.S.C. Appx. §2062(a)(1); Section 2(a)(1) of the DPA.

[3] Congress reauthorized the DPA when it enacted the Defense Production Act Reauthorization of 2009, P.L. 111-67, 123 Stat. 2006-2022.

[4] These changes are discussed at length in this report, but are summarized in **Table A-2** of the Appendix.

[5] Executive Order 13603, "National Defense Resource Preparedness," 77 *Federal Register* 16651, March 22, 2012.

[6] First War Powers Act, 1941 (H.R. 6233, P.L. 77-354, 55 Stat. 838), and Second War Powers Act, 1942 (S. 2208, P.L. 77-507, 56 Stat. 176). The first of these statutes conferred considerable emergency power on the President to reorganize the executive branch, to enter into contracts and make payments on them, and to regulate "trade with the enemy." The second act expanded the powers of the Interstate Commerce Commission to improve the efficiency of transportation of war materials; expanded an existing authority for military departments to acquire private property by condemnation, (continued...)

authority lapsed at the end of that war, but the beginning of the Cold War with the Soviet Union in the late 1940s and the North Korean invasion of South Korea in June of 1950 caused the Truman Administration to reconsider the need for stronger executive authority in the interest of national defense.[7]

A number of factors encouraged President Truman to propose such legislation. Both the armed services and the defense industry supporting the nation's effort during World War II had demobilized during the late 1940s after the cessation of hostilities. With the return of peace, the Administration cut back military expenditures significantly. President Truman accentuated these cuts by placing heavy reliance on atomic weapons to provide for the nation's defense.[8] The perceived power of the atomic arsenal justified, in the eyes of the Administration, substantial cuts in expensive, manpower-intensive conventional military capabilities. This enabled the President to propose and Congress to pass much-reduced defense appropriations.

In addition, the nation had recently experienced substantial economic and industrial turmoil. Demand for housing and consumer products, unleashed by the expiration of wartime economic controls, precipitated a series of postwar labor strikes. These reached their height in 1946 in a nationwide shutdown of passenger and freight rail service, leading President Truman to threaten to seize control of the railways and draft striking rail workers into the Armed Forces, placing them under military discipline. Though the presidential threats were never carried out, the strike served to illustrate the economic context in which the nation approached the Korean War.[9]

(...continued)

purchase, donation, or other transfer; permitted the Secretaries of War and the Navy to place orders and contracts and the President to give such contracts priority over all deliveries for private accounts or for export; and gave the President the authority to require acceptance of and performance under these contracts and to allocate materials and facilities for their fulfillment. The act also empowered the President to obtain information, records, and reports sufficient to enforce the provisions of the act and clarified existing law on the amount of compensation required if property was requisitioned for defense purposes. The act also included provisions relating to free postage for members of the military services, naturalization of persons serving in the armed forces, acceptance of conditional gifts to further the war program, metal content of coinage, inspection and audit of war contractors, and the gathering and assessment of war information by the Department of Commerce.

[7] In a message sent to Congress at the outbreak of war in Korea in mid-1950, President Truman stated that the United States and the United Nations were responding to a military invasion of the Republic of Korea by forces from north of the 38th parallel, that the nation urgently needed additional military manpower, supplies, and equipment, and that the nation's military and economic preparedness were inseparable. He urged Congress to pass legislation that would guarantee the prompt supply of adequate quantities of needed military and civilian goods, including measures to help compensate for manufacturing demand growth caused by military expansion. For more history of the DPA, see U.S. Congress, House Banking and the Currency, *Defense Production Act of 1950*, report to accompany H.R. 9176, 81st Cong., 2nd sess., July 28, 1950, H.Rept. 81-2759 (Washington: GPO, 1950), p. 1.

[8] Examples of the many studies of the impact of atomic weaponry on U.S. strategic thought during the initial years of the Cold War may be found in Edmund Beard, *Developing the ICBM: A Study in Bureaucratic Politics* (New York: Columbia University Press, 1976), pp. 34-35; Bernard Brodie, *Strategy in the Missile Age* (Princeton: Princeton University Press, 1959), pp. 107-144; Harland B. Moulton, "American Strategic Power: Two Decades of Nuclear Strategy and Weapon Systems, 1945-1965" (Ph. D. dissertation, University of Minnesota, 1969), pp. 1-14. A more recent general examination of the development of military strategy during the Truman Administration forms the basis of Patrick W. Steele, "Strategic Air Warfare and Nuclear Strategy: The Formulation of Military Policy in the Truman Administration, 1945-1950" (Ph. D. dissertation, Marquette University, 2010).

[9] See, for example, Robert W. Ruth, "Truman Denies He Gave Ike Order to Take Over in 1946 Railroad Strike," *The Baltimore Sun*, September 19, 1952, p. 1.

The original DPA, enacted on September 8, 1950, granted broad authority to the President to control national economic policy.[10] Containing seven separate titles, the DPA allowed the President, among other powers, to demand that manufacturers give priority to defense production, to requisition materials and property, to expand government and private defense production capacity, to ration consumer goods, to fix wage and price ceilings, to force settlement of some labor disputes, to control consumer credit and regulate real estate construction credit and loans, to provide certain antitrust protections to industry, and to establish a voluntary reserve of private sector executives who would be available for emergency federal employment.

Four of the seven titles (Titles II, IV, V, and VI), which were those related to requisitioning, rationing, wage and price fixing, labor disputes, and credit controls and regulation, terminated in 1953 when Congress allowed them to lapse.[11]

Committee Jurisdiction

Though commonly associated with industrial production for the Department of Defense (DOD), the DPA currently lies within the jurisdiction of the House Committee on Financial Services and the Senate Committee on Banking, Housing, and Urban Affairs. Prior to 1975, House rules did not permit simultaneous referral of bills to two or more committees. Precedents in both chambers did not allow divided or joint referrals, regardless of bill content. Instead, bills were assigned to committees based on the preponderance of their subject matter. Because much of the President's proposal dealt with economic policy, what became the Defense Production Act was assigned in 1950 to the House and Senate Committees on Banking and Currency (their successors are the House Committee on Financial Services and the Senate Committee on Banking, Housing, and Urban Affairs). Although the parts of the act dealing with the requisitioning of materials, wages and prices, labor, and credit are no longer in force, these committees have retained jurisdiction.

In addition to the standing committees of jurisdiction, the original statute created a Joint Committee on Defense Production. This committee was composed of selected members from the standing Committees on Banking and Currency of the Senate and House. This committee was intended to review the programs established by the DPA and advise the standing committees whenever they drafted legislation on the subject. The Joint Committee has not existed, in effect, since 1977 when salaries and expenses for the committee were last funded,[12] although the provision in the DPA establishing the Joint Committee on Defense Production was only officially repealed in 1992.[13]

History of DPA Reauthorizations

The DPA has been amended and reauthorized numerous times since its original enactment. Most notably, with the passage and enactment of P.L. 85-95, Congress reauthorized Titles I, III, and VII

---

[10] P.L. 81-774, 64 Stat. 798.

[11] P.L. 83-95, 67 Stat. 129. P.L. 83-95 permitted the termination of Titles II and VI as of June 30, 1953, and Titles IV and V to terminate as of April 30, 1953.

[12] Although in 1977 Congress extended the 1950 Act through September 30, 1979 (P.L. 95-37), no appropriation for salaries and expenses of the Joint Committee was made for FY1978. The last appropriation for salaries and expenses for the Joint Committee was made in P.L. 94-440.

[13] Section 153 of the Defense Production Act Amendments of 1992 (P.L. 102-558, 106 Stat. 4219).

while allowing Titles II, IV, V, and VI of the DPA to expire in 1953.[14] The Defense Production Act, like the War Power Acts that preceded it, included a sunset provision that has required periodic reauthorization and offered the opportunity for amendment. Congress passed the DPA in 1950 and has thus far reauthorized it 51 times, including many short-term "stop-gap" extensions.[15] From time to time, the DPA has expired without Congress passing a law reauthorizing and extending the termination date of the DPA. However, in such circumstances, Congress has often ultimately passed a law retroactively setting the effective date for the law to the previous expiration date. Most notably, for example, the DPA expired on October 20, 1990, and was not reauthorized until August 17, 1991. However, upon passage of P.L. 102-99, the effective date of the law was set to October 20, 1990.

The DPA was most recently reauthorized by the 111th Congress. Senators Christopher Dodd and Richard Shelby, who were the chairman and ranking Member of the U.S. Senate Committee on Banking, Housing, and Urban Affairs in the 111th Congress, introduced S. 1677, the Defense Production Act Reauthorization of 2009, on September 16, 2009. The bill passed both chambers of Congress by September 23, 2009, and was signed into law by the President as P.L. 111-67 on September 30, 2009.[16]

Most of the authorities of the DPA would have terminated on the day that the reauthorization was signed into law. The Reauthorization of 2009 extended the majority of DPA authorities until September 30, 2014, at which time they will be terminated unless reauthorized once again. For more on the potential termination of DPA authorities after September 30, 2014, see the "Reauthorization of the DPA in the 113th Congress" section in this report.

Major Authorities of the DPA

This section provides summaries of the major authorities granted to the President in the three remaining active Titles of DPA.[17] Each summary describes how the DPA authorities are delegated to Cabinet officials or other offices of the U.S. government in the recently issued Executive Order (E.O.) 13603, *National Defense Resource Preparedness*.[18] The section highlights substantive changes made to these authorities in the Defense Production Act Reauthorization of 2009 (Reauthorization of 2009).[19] This portion of the report identifies substantive changes contained in the Reauthorization of 2009 and E.O. 13603. It is not intended to comprehensively evaluate all authorities in the DPA. The information provided below is reviewed in **Table A-2** in the Appendix for select provisions of the DPA. **Table A-1** also provides a list of additional materials, information, and resources on various topics of the DPA that may be of use to Congress.

---

[14] Act of June 30, 1953, Defense Production Act Amendments of 1953 (S. 1080, P.L. 83-95).

[15] See **Table A-4** in the Appendix for a full chronology of reauthorizations.

[16] The bill was introduced and passed by unanimous consent in the Senate on September 16, 2009. The House passed the bill under the suspension of the rules procedure by voice vote on September 23, 2009.

[17] Titles I, III, and VII. The remaining Titles of the DPA (II, IV, V, and VI) terminated in 1953, but were officially repealed in the Reauthorization of 2009.

[18] Executive Order 13603, "National Defense Resource Preparedness," 77 *Federal Register* 16651, March 22, 2012. E.O. 13603 replaced the previous E.O. 12919 on National Defense Industrial Resource Preparedness, which had been issued by President William J. Clinton on June 3, 1994. See Executive Order 12919, "National Defense Industrial Resources Preparedness," 59 *Federal Register* 29525, June 7, 1994.

[19] P.L. 111-67, Defense Production Act Reauthorization of 2009.

General Scope of the DPA

The DPA provides the President an "array of authorities to shape *national defense* preparedness programs and to take appropriate steps to maintain and enhance the domestic industrial base."[20] [Italics added.] DPA authorities are tied to the definition of *national defense*, as the use of any major DPA authority must be interpreted to promote, support, or otherwise be deemed needed or essential for the national defense.[21] *National defense* is defined in the statute as

> programs for military and energy production or construction, military or critical infrastructure assistance to any foreign nation, homeland security, stockpiling, space, and any directly related activity. Such term includes emergency preparedness activities conducted pursuant to title VI of The Robert T. Stafford Disaster Relief and Emergency Assistance Act [42 U.S.C. §5195 et seq.] and critical infrastructure protection and restoration.[22]

Further reference can be made to Title VI of the Stafford Act for a definition of "emergency preparedness" activities. It states that emergency preparedness:

> means all those activities and measures designed or undertaken to prepare for or minimize the effects of a hazard upon the civilian population, to deal with the immediate emergency conditions which would be created by the hazard, and to effectuate emergency repairs to, or the emergency restoration of, vital utilities and facilities destroyed or damaged by the hazard.[23]

Therefore, the use of DPA authorities extends beyond shaping U.S. military preparedness and capabilities, as the authorities may also be used to enhance and support domestic preparedness, response, and recovery from hazards, terrorist attacks, and other national emergencies, among other purposes.

In its original 1950 form, the DPA defined *national defense* as "the operations and activities of the armed forces, the Atomic Energy Commission, or any other department or agency directly or indirectly and substantially concerned with the national defense...."[24] Over the many reauthorizations and amendments to the DPA, Congress has gradually expanded the scope of the definition of national defense, and did so again in 2009.[25] At that time, Congress included critical infrastructure assistance to any foreign nation and added homeland security to the definition.[26]

---

[20] 50 U.S.C. Appx. §2062(a)(4); Section 2(a)(4) of the DPA (emphasis added).

[21] There are various ties to national defense throughout the DPA. Some examples: Title I, Section 101 priorities and allocations authority requires the President to deem action as "necessary or appropriate to promote the national defense" (50 U.S.C. Appx. §2071(a)); Title III authorities can be used when "essential for the national defense" (50 U.S.C. Appx. §§2091(a), 2092(a), 2093(a)); and Title VII voluntary agreement authority requires that the use helps "provide for the national defense" (50 U.S.C. Appx. §2158(c)(1)).

[22] 50 U.S.C. Appx. §2152(14); Section 702(14) of the DPA.

[23] 42 U.S.C. §5195(a)(3)

[24] See Section 702(d) of P.L. 81-774.

[25] For further discussion of the evolution of the definition of national defense, see The National Infrastructure Advisory Council, *Framework for Dealing with Disasters and Related Interdependencies: Final Report and Recommendations*, Appendix G: The Defense Production Act, Washington, D.C., July 14, 2009, pp. 41-42, at http://www.dhs.gov/xlibrary/assets/niac/niac_framework_dealing_with_disasters.pdf.

[26] 123 Stat. 2017, Section 8 of P.L. 111-67. Both "critical infrastructure" and "homeland security" are defined in Section 702 of the DPA, 50 U.S.C. Appx. §2152.

For more on the other definition changes to the DPA in the Reauthorization of 2009, see the section "Definitions of Key Terms in the DPA" of this report.

The DPA also includes a full statement of policy and congressional findings, as set forth in the "Declaration of Policy."[27] In 2009, Congress amended the declaration of policy by expanding the text to explicitly list natural disasters and terrorist attacks as being part of the national defense.[28] The declaration was also amended to include "biomass" and "more efficient energy storage and distribution technologies" as forms of renewable energy to augment domestic energy supplies to further assure the adequate maintenance of the domestic industrial base.[29] The Reauthorization of 2009 also often reordered or slightly reworded various clauses.

Authorities under Title I of the DPA

Priorities and Allocations Authority

Section 101(a) of Title I of the DPA states:

> The President is authorized (1) to require that performance under contracts or orders (other than contracts of employment) which he deems necessary or appropriate to promote the national defense shall take priority over performance under any other contract or order, and, for the purpose of assuring such priority, to require acceptance and performance of such contracts or orders in preference to other contracts or orders by any person he finds to be capable of their performance, and (2) to allocate materials, services, and facilities in such manner, upon such conditions, and to such extent as he shall deem necessary or appropriate to promote the national defense.[30]

The *priority* performance authority allows the federal government to ensure the timely availability of critical materials, equipment, and services produced in the private market in the interest of national defense, and to receive those materials, equipment, and services through contracts before any other competing interest.[31] Under the language of the DPA, a *person*

---

[27] 50 U.S.C. Appx. §2062; Section 2 of the DPA. This section comprises congressional findings, Section 2(a), and a statement of policy of the United States, Section 2(b).

[28] For instance, in Section 2(a)(1), Congress now finds that "the security of the United States is dependent on the ability of the domestic industrial base to supply materials and services for the national defense and *to prepare for and respond to military conflicts, natural or man-caused disasters, or acts of terrorism within the United States*". [Italics added.] Additionally, the Reauthorization of 2009 added Section 2(b)(5), which states "authorities under this Act [50 U.S.C. App. §§2061-2171] should be used to reduce the vulnerability of the United States to terrorist attacks, and to minimize the damage and assist in the recovery from terrorist attacks that occur in the United States." 123 Stat. 2007, Section 3 of P.L. 111-67.

[29] In the 2009 reauthorization of the DPA, an existing provision in the declaration of policy was amended to state that "to further assure the adequate maintenance of the domestic industrial base, to the maximum extent possible, domestic energy supplies should be augmented through reliance on renewable energy sources (including solar, geothermal, wind, and *biomass* sources), *more efficient energy storage and distribution technologies*, and energy conservation measures" [italics added for new text]. See 123 Stat. 2007, Section 3 of P.L. 111-67 and the current 50 U.S.C. Appx. .§2062(a)(6); Section 2(a)(6) of the DPA.

In other words, under this declaration of policy, Congress has found that it is in the interest of national defense preparedness that the government assure some level capacity exists in the domestic industrial base to produce and provide renewable energy sources, including from biomass sources.

[30] 50 U.S.C. Appx. §2071(a); Section 101(a) of the DPA.

[31] As noted in regulations for Title I authorities, especially 15 C.F.R. §700.1(b), this priority authority is broader than (continued...)

(including corporations, as defined in statute)[32] is required to accept prioritized contracts/orders,[33] though regulations implementing Title I authorities provide practical exemptions to this mandate. The limited allowances for when a person is required to or may optionally reject a prioritized order can be superseded by the direction of the implementing federal department.[34] In executing a contract under the DPA, a contractor is not liable for actions taken to comply with governing rules, regulations, and orders (e.g., prioritization requirements), including any rules, regulations, or orders later declared legally invalid.[35] The government can also prioritize the performance of contracts between two private parties, such as a contract between a prime contractor and a subcontractor, if needed to fulfill a priority contract and promote the national defense.[36]

Title I also allows the President to *allocate* or control the general distribution of materials, services, and facilities. Allocation authority relates historically to the controlled materials programs of World War II, when the distribution of critical materials and resources had to be managed to maximize the production of goods needed in the war effort.[37] This authority is rarely used today, and is currently only implemented for the Civil Reserve Air Fleet (CRAF) program, under which the DOD may augment its airlift capability with civilian aircraft during a national defense related crisis.[38]

There are several notable restrictions to the priorities and allocation authority. For example, it cannot be used for contracts of employment.[39] Additionally, unless authorized by a joint resolution of Congress, the authority cannot be used for wage or price controls. Private persons are not required to assist in the production or development of chemical or biological weapons unless directly authorized by the President or a Cabinet secretary.[40]

(...continued)

similar priority authorities provided in other statutes including Section 18 of the Selective Service Act of 1948 (50 U.S.C. Appx. §468).

[32] 50 U.S.C. Appx. §2152(15), Section 702(15) of the DPA, defines person as "individual, corporation, partnership, association, or any other organized group of persons, or legal successor or representative thereof, or any State or local government or agency thereof."

[33] Contracts and "rated orders" have the same meaning in the regulations on Title I authorities, see, for example, the definition for "rated order" provided by 15 C.F.R. §700.8.

[34] See, for example, the regulations establishing standards and procedures for the use of the Secretaries' of Commerce, Energy, and Transportation delegated authorities under Title I of the DPA (15 C.F.R. §700.13, 10 C.F.R. §217.33, and 49 C.F.R. §33.33, respectively). These regulations explain the circumstances a person may reject a prioritized contract, though these conditions are limited by the clause "Unless otherwise directed by the [implementing department]."

[35] 50 U.S.C. Appx. §2157; Section 707 of the DPA. Immunity under this provision is limited, and does not confer blanket tort immunity to a contractor for liability to injured third parties. Also, carrying out a contract according to its terms does not necessarily entitle a contractor to be indemnified by the government when the resulting product injures third parties, absent an indemnification clause in the contract. Hercules v. United States, 516 U.S. 417 (1996).

[36] See, for example, 15 C.F.R. §700.3(d).

[37] See further explanation of allocation authority in 15 C.F.R. §700.30(a)(2). In a proposed rulemaking that would revise current regulations issued by the Department of Commerce with regards to priorities and allocations authority, the proposed definition of allocation is: "The control of the distribution of materials, services, or facilities for a purpose deemed necessary or appropriate to promote the national defense." See Department of Commerce, "Revisions to Defense Priorities and Allocations System Regulations," 79 *Federal Register* 5332, January 31, 2014.

[38] Department of Homeland Security, *The Defense Production Act Committee: Report to Congress*, August 2011, p. 9. For more on the CRAF program, see http://www.dot.gov/ost/oiser/craf.htm.

[39] This restriction is written as a parenthetical in Section 101(a)(1), but is an important constraint on Title I priorities authority.

[40] 50 U.S.C. Appx. §2074; Section 104 of the DPA. It should be noted that development and production of chemical (continued...)

Determinations and Delegations

In statute, Title I priorities and allocation authority can only be used to "promote national defense." In E.O. 13603, the President further constrains that authority so that it "may be used only to support programs that have been determined in writing as necessary or appropriate to promote the national defense" by the either the Secretary of Defense, the Secretary of Homeland Security, or the Secretary of Energy, depending on the issue involved.[41] Once a program is determined to promote the national defense, other Secretaries who have been delegated the priorities and allocation authority can use their authority for those pre-designated program purposes.

E.O. 13603 provides for the delegation of the President's priorities and allocation authority to six different Cabinet Secretaries based upon their areas of expertise in different resource and material sectors. These resource areas are further defined in Section 801 of E.O. 13603. The delegation to the Cabinet Secretaries in E.O. 13603 did not differ from the earlier executive order, though the definitions of their assigned resource areas did change somewhat. **Table A-3** in the Appendix summarizes this delegation of priorities and allocation authority.

How Priorities and Allocations Changed in the Reauthorization of 2009 and E.O. 13603

The statutory language providing Section 101(a) priorities and allocation authority has existed, unaltered, since the original enactment of the DPA.[42] However, in the Reauthorization of 2009, Congress added a rulemaking requirement to the statute. Congress mandated that all Cabinet Secretaries delegated priorities and allocation authority establish standards and procedures for its use. The statute further encourages these rules to be consistent and unified in nature, a recommendation made by the Government Accountability Office and endorsed by the reauthorization bill's principal sponsor.[43]

(...continued)

weapons and biological weapons are prohibited by the Chemical Weapons Convention (CWC) and the Biological Weapons Convention (BWC), respectively. The United States is a state party to both of these international treaties and is legally bound by their obligations and prohibitions.

[41] See Section 202 of E.O. 13603. Determinations are made

> (a) by the Secretary of Defense with respect to military production and construction, military assistance to foreign nations, military use of civil transportation, stockpiles managed by the Department of Defense, space, and directly related activities; (b) by the Secretary of Energy with respect to energy production and construction, distribution and use, and directly related activities; and (c) by the Secretary of Homeland Security with respect to all other national defense programs, including civil defense and continuity of Government.

In practice, some determination authority has been further re-delegated within the executive branch. An example of a written determination, issued by the Department of Homeland Security through FEMA, can be found at http://www.fema.gov/pdf/about/programs/dpa/signed-program-determinations-100506.pdf.

[42] See Section 101 of P.L. 81-774.

[43] See 50 U.S.C. Appx. §2071(d); Section 101(d) of the DPA and U.S. Government Accountability Office, *Defense Production Act: Agencies Lack Policies and Guidance for Use of Key Authorities*, GAO-08-854, June 2008, at http://www.gao.gov/products/GAO-08-854. Sen. Christopher Dodd, "Defense Production Act Reauthorization of 2009," Senate consideration of S. 1677, *Congressional Record*, September 16, 2009, p. S9480.

The necessary rules were required to be issued within 270 days from bill enactment, or the end of June 2010. Of the six departments delegated authority, three (Commerce, Energy, and Transportation) had issued final rules as of June 10, 2014. Though it has been periodically updated to conform to evolving practices and DPA statute, the Department of Commerce's (DOC's) rule establishing the Defense Priorities and Allocations System (DPAS) has existed in its current basic format since 1984.[44] DOC is currently updating the DPAS to account for the Reauthorization of 2009.[45] The Department of Agriculture has also issued a proposed rule. The Departments of Defense and Health and Human Services have not yet released rules in proposed or final form.[46]

Examples of Use

The allocation authority has rarely been used by the government, but the authority to prioritize contracts is routinely employed by the DOD. In a typical year, DOD will assign a DPA priority to more than 300,000 contracts, representing more than 20% of the nearly 1.5 million contracts reported by the department and its subordinate military departments, agencies, and offices for FY2012.[47] These prioritized contracts are typically issued under the DOC's delegated authority with respect to materials, services, and facilities, including construction materials, and under its regulations guiding the use of this authority.[48] Some notable examples of DOD's use of Title I priorities authority include supporting the development of the Integrated Ballistic Missile Defense System and Mine Resistant Ambush Protected (MRAP) Vehicles.[49] While the priorities authority is used far less frequently by other departments and agencies, it has been used for both the

---

[44] For original rulemaking of the Defense Priorities and Allocations System, see Department of Commerce, "Defense Priorities and Allocations System," 49 *Federal Register* 30412, July 30, 1984. Prior to the DPAS, DOC maintained a "Defense Materials System" and a "Defense Priorities System" that were superseded by the DPAS.

[45] DOC has twice proposed to revise its DPAS rule in accordance with the Reauthorization of 2009. It first proposed a rulemaking that would revise this existing regulation in June of 2010, but this proposal was never finalized. See Department of Commerce, "Revisions to Defense Priorities and Allocations System Regulations," 75 *Federal Register* 32122, June 7, 2010. However, on January 31, 2014, the DOC replaced this proposal with another, different proposed revision. As noted in the current proposed rulemaking, the original "June 2010 proposed rule would have substantially reorganized the format of the DPAS. This [current] proposed rule would largely retain the existing format." See Department of Commerce, "Revisions to Defense Priorities and Allocations System Regulations," 79 *Federal Register* 5353, January 31, 2014.

[46] The Department of Agriculture has a proposed rulemaking that has not been finalized, see Department of Agriculture, "Agriculture Priorities and Allocations System," 76 *Federal Register* 29084, May 19, 2011. The Department of Energy issued a final rule codified in 10 C.F.R. Part 217, see Department of Energy, "Energy Priorities and Allocations System Regulations," 75 *Federal Register* 41405, July 16, 2010. The Department of Transportation issued a final rule codified in 49 C.F.R. Part 33, see Department of Transportation, "Prioritization and Allocation Authority Exercised by the Secretary of Transportation Under the Defense Production Act," 77 *Federal Register* 59793, October 1, 2012. The Administration has reported that new rules are being prepared by the Department of Agriculture and the Department of Health and Human Services, but did not mention the development of a rule by the Department of Defense. See Department of Homeland Security, *The Defense Production Act Committee: Report to Congress*, March 31, 2013, p. 4.

[47] Department of Homeland Security, *The Defense Production Act Committee: Report to Congress*, August 2011, p. 7. Total contract data for FY2012 compiled from USASpending.gov on May 17, 2013.

[48] Ibid. DOD has been re-delegated authority by DOC to use their regulations and authorities for Title I priorities authority.

[49] There are two levels of priority rating provided in DPAS regulations. The "DO" rating is lower than a "DX" rating. For a discussion of the different priority ratings, see 15 C.F.R. §700.11. DOD, as a matter of practice, includes a DO rating on most commercial contracts. Only select programs may receive a "DX" rating. For a current list of "DX" rated programs, see http://www.bis.doc.gov/dpas/pdfdocs/list_of_dx_approved_programs.pdf.

prevention of terrorism and natural disaster preparedness. For example, the Federal Bureau of Investigation has prioritized contracts in support of the Terrorist Screening Center program and the U.S. Army Corps of Engineers prioritized contracts in support of the Greater New Orleans Hurricane and Storm Damage Risk Reduction System program.[50]

Title I and Energy

Title I also contains several provisions related to domestic energy. Section 101(c) authorizes the President to allocate and prioritize contracts for materials, equipment, and services to maximize domestic energy supplies in certain circumstances.[51] This authority was used by the Department of Energy to ensure that emergency supplies of natural gas continued to flow to California utilities, helping to avoid threatened electrical blackouts in early 2001.[52] However, Section 105 of the DPA restricts its authorities from being used to ration the end-use of gasoline without the approval of Congress.

Section 106 of Title I, as amended, also designates *energy* as a *strategic and critical* material.[53] This designation enables other authorities in the DPA, especially Title III authorities discussed below, to be used for policy decisions related to energy. However, prior to the Reauthorization of 2009, the DPA did *not* grant any new direct or indirect authority to the President to "engage in the production of energy in any manner whatsoever (such as oil and gas exploration and development, or any energy facility construction), except as expressly provided in sections 305 and 306 [50 U.S.C. App. §§2095 and 2096] for synthetic fuel production."[54] This restriction designating "energy" as "strategic and critical material" was deleted in Section 5 of the Reauthorization of 2009.[55] With that restriction eliminated, the specific exemption for synthetic fuel production became unnecessary, so the Reauthorization of 2009 also repealed several sections on the production of synthetic fuel.[56] The issue of synthetic fuel production and the use of the DPA for energy production has an extensive history that is beyond the scope of this report.[57]

Authorities Under Title III of the DPA

Title III authorities are intended to help ensure that the nation has an adequate supply of, or the ability to produce, essential materials and goods necessary for the national defense. Using Title III authorities, the President may provide appropriate financial incentives to develop, maintain, modernize, restore, and expand the production capacity of domestic sources for critical

---

[50] Department of Homeland Security, *The Defense Production Act Committee: Report to Congress*, August 2011, p. 8.

[51] 50 U.S.C. Appx. §2071(c); Section 101(c) of the DPA.

[52] For discussion on how DPA was used in this situation, see U.S. Congress, Senate Committee on Banking, Housing, and Urban Affairs, *California Energy Crisis and Use of the Defense Production Act*, 107th Cong., 1st sess., February 9, 2001, S. Hrg. 107-215 (Washington: GPO, 2001).

[53] 50 U.S.C. Appx. §2076; Section 106 of the DPA.

[54] See the former 50 U.S.C. Appx. §2076(2) [2006 edition]

[55] 123 Stat. 2009.

[56] See 50 U.S.C. Appx. §2095 to §2098 [2006 edition]; the former sections 306, 307, and 308 of the DPA.

[57] In brief, these DPA authorities supported the Synthetic Fuels Corporation, established in P.L. 96-294. Language rescinding most of the Synthetic Fuels Corporation funding was included in the FY1986 continuing appropriations resolution (H.J.Res. 465, P.L. 99-190).

components, critical technology items, materials, and industrial resources essential for the execution of the national security strategy of the United States.[58] The President is also directed to use Title III authorities to ensure that critical components, critical technology items, essential materials, and industrial resources are available from reliable sources when needed to meet defense requirements during peacetime, graduated mobilization, and national emergency.[59] In the Reauthorization of 2009, Congress amended and replaced the full text of Title III, though the core purpose and content of the authorities remain principally the same.[60] From an administrative standpoint, language was updated throughout Title III to comply with more modern legislative style and structure.

Loan Guarantees and Direct Loans

Sections 301 and 302 of Title III of the DPA authorize the President to issue loan guarantees and direct loans to reduce current or projected shortfalls of industrial resources, critical technology items, or essential materials needed for national defense purposes.[61] Loan guarantees and direct loans can be issued to private businesses to help them create, maintain, expedite, expand, protect, or restore production and deliveries or services essential to the national defense.[62] A direct loan is a loan from the federal government to another government or private sector borrower that requires repayment, with or without interest. A loan guarantee allows the federal government to guarantee a loan made by a non-federal lender to a non-federal borrower, either by pledging to pay back all or part of the loan in the instance that the borrower is unable to do so.[63] These authorities, for instance, could be used to provide a loan, or to guarantee a loan, to a defense contractor that is responsible for the provision of critical services essential to the national defense when credit is otherwise unavailable in the private market.

How Loan Authority Changed in the Reauthorization of 2009

According to Senator Christopher J. Dodd of Connecticut, the reauthorization bill's principal sponsor, the loan authorities provided in Sections 301 and 302 were updated in order to comply with the Federal Credit Reform Act of 1990.[64] In general, these changes increased restrictions on the use of the authority by the President. For example, prior to the Reauthorization of 2009, Section 301 and 302 authorized the President to make loans and loan guarantees if an "industrial resource shortfall," which the direct loan or loan guarantee was intended to correct, had been identified in the President's annual budget submission to Congress (or amendment to the submission).[65] Since reauthorization, the budget authority for guarantees and direct loans must be

---

[58] 50 U.S.C. Appx. §2077; Section 107(a) of the DPA. Many of these terms are defined further in 50 U.S.C. Appx. §2152.

[59] 50 U.S.C. Appx. §2077; Section 107(b)(1) of the DPA.

[60] 123 Stat. 2010-2017.

[61] 50 U.S.C. Appx. §2091(a)(1). The beginning of 50 U.S.C. Appx. §2092(a) includes the same basic text as §2091(a)(1).

[62] Ibid.

[63] For more on direct loans and loan guarantees, see CRS Report R42632, *Budgetary Treatment of Federal Credit (Direct Loans and Loan Guarantees): Concepts, History, and Issues for Congress*.

[64] Sen. Christopher Dodd, "Defense Production Act Reauthorization of 2009," Senate consideration of S. 1677, *Congressional Record*, September 16, 2009, p. S9481.

[65] See former 50 U.S.C. Appx. §2091(e)(1)(A) and 50 U.S.C. Appx. §2092(c)(1) [2006 edition].

specifically included in appropriations passed by Congress and enacted by the President before they can be issued.[66] Both before and after 2009, the President is allowed to waive the majority of restrictions on use of this authority during periods of national emergency declared by the President or Congress.[67]

Except in declared national emergencies, this statute also requires the President to determine that loan guarantees or direct loans meet a number of conditions before issuance. Perhaps most importantly, one of the conditions in using the loan authority is that the loan or loan guarantee is the most cost-effective, expedient, and practical alternative method for meeting the need.[68] Prior to the reauthorization, the President had been required to determine that the ability of domestic industrial sources to produce a good or service was insufficient to meet the combined projected defense and non-defense demand.[69] In other words, the President had been required to determine that there was an insufficient supply of a good before issuing a loan guarantee or direct loan. The Reauthorization of 2009 removed this requirement, but expanded the determination requirements for guarantee and direct loans to include provisions that may help ensure that the loan is repaid by the recipient.[70] For example, the President is now required to determine that there is "reasonable assurance" that a recipient of a loan or loan guarantee will be able to repay the loan.[71]

Purchase, Purchase Commitments, and Installation of Equipment

Section 303 of Title III grants the President an array of authorities to create, maintain, protect, expand, or restore domestic industrial base capabilities essential to the national defense.[72] These authorities include, but are not limited to:

- purchasing or making purchase commitments of industrial resources or critical technology items;[73]

- making subsidized payments for domestically produced materials; and[74]

- installing and purchasing equipment for industrial facilities to expand their productive capacity.[75]

In general, Section 303 authorities can be used by the President to provide incentives for domestic private industry to produce and supply critical goods that are necessary for the national defense.

---

[66] 50 U.S.C. Appx. §2091(a)(3) and 50 U.S.C. Appx. §2092(c).

[67] See former 50 U.S.C. Appx. §2091(a)(3) and 50 U.S.C. Appx. §2092(b)(2) [2006 edition]; and current 50 U.S.C. Appx. §2091(a)(2) and 50 U.S.C. Appx. §2092(b)(2).

[68] 50 U.S.C. Appx. §2091(a)(2)(C) and 50 U.S.C. Appx. §2092(b)(2)(C).

[69] See former 50 U.S.C. Appx. §2091(a)(3)(D) and 50 U.S.C. Appx. §2092(b)(2)(D) [2006 edition].

[70] The Reauthorization of 2009 added 50 U.S.C. Appx. §§2091(a)(2)(D), (E), and (F) and 50 U.S.C. Appx. §§2092(b)(2)(D) and (E); which are Sections 301(a)(2)(D), (E), and (F) and Sections 302(b)(2)(D) and (E) of the DPA, respectively.

[71] See 50 U.S.C. Appx. §§2091(a)(2)(D), Section 301(a)(2)(D) of the DPA.

[72] 50 U.S.C. Appx. §2093, Section 303 of the DPA.

[73] 50 U.S.C. Appx. §2093(a), Section 303(a)(1)(A) of the DPA. The terms "critical technology item" and "industry resource" are further defined in 50 U.S.C. Appx. §2152, Section 702 of the DPA.

[74] 50 U.S.C. Appx. §2093(c), Section 303(c) of the DPA.

[75] 50 U.S.C. Appx. §2093(e), Section 303(e) of the DPA.

The scope of Section 303 authorities allows for these incentives to be structured in a number of ways, including direct purchases or subsidies of such goods.

Determination and Notification of an Industrial Base Shortfall

Prior to using Section 303 authorities, the law requires the President to determine that there is a "domestic industrial base shortfall" for a particular industrial resource, material, or critical technology item that threatens the national defense.[76] This determination includes finding that the industry of the United States cannot reasonably be expected to provide the capability for the good in a timely manner.[77] The President is required to notify the committees of jurisdiction when such a determination is made and give the committees 30 days to comment if the cost of actions to remedy the shortfall is expected to exceed $50 million.[78] The President is authorized to waive the determination and notification provisions in periods of national emergency or in situations that the President, on a non-delegable basis, determines the industrial base shortfall would severely impair national defense.[79]

How Section 303 Authority Changed in the Reauthorization of 2009

Expansion of Authorities

Section 303(a)(1) of DPA provides an "In general" list of actions the President may take in order to meet the needs of the national defense. In the Reauthorization of 2009, Congress clarified the President's authority in Section 303(a)(1) to specifically state that the authorities may be used to "create, maintain, protect, expand, or restart domestic industrial base capabilities."[80] Previously, this section only stated that the authorities could "assist in carrying out the objectives" of the DPA.[81] More significantly, the Reauthorization of 2009 also expanded the list of authorized actions in the Section 303(a)(1) subsection to include providing for the "development of production capabilities" and "for the increased use of emerging technologies in security program applications and the rapid transition of emerging technologies."[82]

Likewise, Section 303(e) has long authorized the President to enhance productive capacity by directly procuring and installing manufacturing equipment in both government and privately owned industrial facilities. In the reauthorization, this authority was expanded to allow the President to provide for the modification or expansion of privately owned facilities, as well as the ability to sell and transfer equipment to privately owned industrial facilities.[83] In addition, the statute now requires that the owner of an industrial facility receiving equipment from this

---

[76] The President delegated authority to make these determinations to the "head of each agency engage[d] in procurement for national defense" in Section 305(b) of E.O. 13603. Section 303(a)(5) of the DPA states that an "industrial base shortfall" exists when domestic industry "cannot be reasonably expected to provide the capability for the need."

[77] 50 U.S.C. Appx. §2093(a)(5)(B), Section 303(a)(5)(B) of the DPA.

[78] 50 U.S.C. Appx. §2093(a)(6), Section 303(a)(6) of the DPA

[79] 50 U.S.C. Appx. §2093(a)(7), Section 303(a)(7) of the DPA.

[80] 50 U.S.C. Appx. §2093(a)(1), Section 303(a)(1) of the DPA

[81] See the former 50 U.S.C. Appx §2093(a)(1) [2006 Edition], what was 303(a)(1) of the DPA.

[82] 50 U.S.C. Appx. §§2093(a)(1)(C) and (D), Section 303(a)(1)(C) and (D) of the DPA; 123 Stat 2014.

[83] 50 U.S.C. Appx. §§2093(e)(1)(C) and (D), Section 303(e)(1)(C) and (D) of the DPA.

subsection of authorities indemnify the federal government from certain liability claims under the Comprehensive Environmental Response, Compensation, and Liability Act of 1980.[84]

Determination and Notification Requirements

While the Reauthorization of 2009 tightened restrictions on the use of Sections 301 and 302, it appears to have eased the use of Section 303 authorities. In order to use Section 303 authorities the President is required to make a determination that there is a "domestic industrial base shortfall" of a particular good before initiating action under the section. Prior to being struck from the statute by the 2009 reauthorization, the President's determination requirement under this section also included the conditions that

> purchases, purchase commitments, or other action pursuant to this section are the most cost effective, expedient, and practical alternative method for meeting the need; and

> the combination of the United States national defense demand and foreseeable nondefense demand for the industrial resource or critical technology item is not less than the output of domestic industrial capability, as determined by the President, including the output to be established through the purchase, purchase commitment, or other action.[85]

However, these two conditions were struck from the statute in the Reauthorization of 2009. In addition, the law previously contained a limitation on the amount of money that could be spent on actions to rectify a domestic industrial base shortfall. Prior to 2009, the actions that would cause aggregate spending in excess of $50 million needed to be specifically authorized by law.[86] This was changed in the reauthorization, and the President is now allowed to initiate actions in aggregate of over $50 million after a waiting period of 30 days following notification to the committees of jurisdiction.[87]

Delegation of Section 301, 302, and 303 Authorities in E.O. 13603

In E.O. 13603, the "head of each agency engaged in procurement for national defense" is delegated the majority of the authorities of Sections 301, 302, and 303 of Title III of the DPA.[88] These agencies are specifically identified in E.O. 13603.[89] This delegation includes the ability to make all determinations not explicitly cited in the statute as being nondelegable.[90] However, this

---

[84] Specifically, 50 U.S.C. Appx. §2093(e)(2), Section 303(e)(2) of the DPA requires owners to waive claims against the United States under Section 107 or 113 of CERCLA. For more on these liabilities, see CRS Report R41039, *Comprehensive Environmental Response, Compensation, and Liability Act: A Summary of Superfund Cleanup Authorities and Related Provisions of the Act*, by David M. Bearden.

[85] See former 50 U.S.C. Appx §§2093(a)(5)(C) and (D) [2006 Edition]. They were deleted from law in Section 7 of P.L. 111-67, 123 Stat. 2014.

[86] See former 50 U.S.C. Appx §§2093(a)(6)(C) [2006 Edition].

[87] 50 U.S.C. Appx §§2093(a)(6)(B), Section 303(a)(6)(B) of the DPA.

[88] See Sections 301, 302, 303, 304, and 305 of E.O. 13603.

[89] Section 801(h) of E.O. 13603 states "the heads of the Departments of State, Justice, the Interior, and Homeland Security, the Office of the Director of National Intelligence, the Central Intelligence Agency, the National Aeronautics and Space Administration, the General Services Administration, and all other agencies with authority delegated under section 201 of this order." Under Section 201 of the executive order, the additional agencies are the Departments of Agriculture, Commerce, Defense, Energy, Health and Human Services, and Transportation.

[90] Section 305 of E.O. 13603. The only determination not delegable is 50 U.S.C. Appx. §2093(a)(7)(B), Section 303(a)(7)(B) of the DPA. This determination allows the President, on a non-delegable basis, to waive requirements in (continued...)

---

delegation does not include the authority to encourage the exploration, development, and mining of strategic and critical materials and other materials. This authority is provided to the President in the statute, and is delegated only to the Secretaries of Defense and the Interior.[91]

E.O. 13603 offers a level of uniformity and clarity to the delegation of Title III authorities that was absent from previous executive orders. Under an earlier executive order that implemented the pre-2009 DPA, authorities had been delegated through a similar definition process, but were additionally tied to another executive order. The additional step of referring to another executive order for delegations was eliminated in E.O. 13603.[92]

Use of Title III Authorities

According to the Defense Production Act Committee, the federal government has not used the loan authorities provided in Section 301 or Section 302 of Title III in more than 30 years. Rather, current projects are initiated under Section 303 of Title III of the DPA.[93] There are approximately 28 current Title III research or procurement projects that are "focused on ensuring future U.S. production capabilities and maintaining U.S. technological leadership in critical markets."[94] Examples include a "Lithium Ion Battery Production for Space Applications" and a "Lightweight Ammunition Production Initiative."[95] These examples, like many other Title III projects, are meant to establish a domestic capacity to produce these advanced technologies deemed essential for national defense.

Defense Production Act Fund

The DPA contains a blanket authorization of appropriations needed to carry out all of its provisions and purposes.[96] Title III of the DPA also establishes a Treasury account, the Defense Production Act Fund, that is available to carry out all of the provisions and purposes of Title III. The monies in the DPA Fund are available until expended. The DPA Fund is also used to collect all proceeds from DPA activities under Title III, such as the resale of DPA-procured commodities or products.[97] However, the balance in the DPA Fund at the end of any fiscal year cannot exceed $750 million, excluding monies appropriated for that fiscal year or obligated amounts.[98] The only

---

(...continued)

Section 303(a)(1)-(6) on the use of those authorities.

[91] In statute, see 50 U.S.C. Appx. §2093(a)(1)(B); Section 303(a)(1)(B) of the DPA. The authority is delegated in Section 306 of E.O. 13603. The Secretary of Interior is delegated this authority in consultation with the Secretary of Defense, as the National Defense Stockpile Manager.

[92] See the definition for "head of each agency engaged in procurement for national defense" in Section 802(h) of E.O. 12919, which had been issued on June 3, 1994.

[93] Department of Homeland Security, *The Defense Production Act Committee: Report to Congress*, August 2011, p. 10. For a current list of all DPA Title III projects, see http://www.dpatitle3.com/dpa_db/.

[94] Ibid.

[95] See http://www.dpatitle3.com/dpa_db/project.php?id=67 and http://www.dpatitle3.com/dpa_db/project.php?id=66, respectively.

[96] 50 U.S.C. Appx. §2161; Section 711 of the DPA. This section will terminate on September 14, 2014, unless reauthorized.

[97] 50 U.S.C. Appx. §2094; Section 304 of the DPA.

[98] 50 U.S.C. Appx. §2094(e); Section 304(e) of the DPA. The obligation of funds is defined in the DOD Financial Management Regulation as an "amount representing orders placed, contracts awarded, services received, and similar (continued...)

---

substantive change made to the DPA Fund in the Reauthorization of 2009 was to increase this allowable annual balance for the Fund from $400 million to $750 million.[99] **Table 1** provides the appropriations to the DPA Fund between FY2010 and FY2014. It is possible for appropriations to the DPA Fund to be made in any of the bills providing funding to the numerous agencies delegated Title III authorities.[100] However, all recent direct appropriations to the DPA Fund have come from appropriation bills for the Department of Defense (or the relevant division of an omnibus appropriations bill). Distinctively, as noted in **Table 1**, in FY2014, the Department of Energy has been authorized to transfer up to $45 million to the DPA Fund from the overall appropriation to another account.[101]

Table 1. Appropriations to the DPA Fund Since FY2010, in Millions

Fiscal Year	Law	Appropriation Amount
2010	P.L. 111-118, 123 Stat. 3422	$150.7
2011	P.L. 112-10, 125 Stat. 51	$34.3
2012	P.L. 112-74, 125 Stat. 800	$170.0
2013	P.L. 113-6, 127 Stat. 291	$223.5
2014	P.L. 113-76, 128 Stat. 98	$60.1[a]

Source: CRS analysis of appropriation acts. Dollars rounded to the nearest hundred thousand. These figures may not account for transfers or other obligations to the DPA Fund and may not reflect adjustments to appropriations required by recently enacted legislation.

a. P.L. 113-76, 128 Stat. 165, also authorizes the Department of Energy to transfer up to $45 million to the DPA Fund from the overall appropriation of $1,912 million for the Energy Efficiency and Renewable Energy account.

The President is also required to designate a "Fund manager" to carry out general accounting functions for the fund.[102] The Secretary of Defense has been delegated this responsibility in E.O. 13603.[103] As the Fund Manager, the Secretary of Defense (or official to whom the authority is delegated) is responsible for the financial accounting of the fund, but does not necessarily have decision-making authority over the use of the fund. The designation of a Fund Manager did not change from E.O. 12919, as amended.

(...continued)

transactions during an accounting period that will require payment during the same, or a future, period." Office of the Comptroller, Department of Defense, *Financial Management Regulation*, DOD 7000.14-R, Washington, DC, December 2008, p. Glossary-21.

[99] 123 Stat. 2017.

[100] See footnote 89 for an explanation and full list of the delegated agencies with Title III authorities.

[101] In its FY2014 President's budget request, DOE stated the $45 million would be used to support a joint DOD-Navy, DOE, and USDA memorandum of agreement to support the construction of commercial-scale biofuels production facilities that can produce drop-in, hydrocarbon biofuels. For more information on the memorandum of understanding, see CRS Report R42859, *DOD Alternative Fuels: Policy, Initiatives and Legislative Activity*, by Katherine Blakeley, and CRS Report R42568, *The Navy Biofuel Initiative Under the Defense Production Act*, by Anthony Andrews et al.

[102] 50 U.S.C. Appx. §2094(f); Section 304(f) of the DPA.

[103] Section 309 of E.O. 13603.

Authorities Under Title VII of the DPA

Title VII of the DPA contains an assorted mix of provisions that clarify how DPA authorities should and can be used, as well as additional presidential authorities. Significant provisions of Title VII, and how they have changed under the Reauthorization of 2009 or how delegations of the authority changed with the issuance of E.O. 13603, are summarized here.

Special Preference for Small Businesses

There are two provisions in the DPA directing the President to accord special preference to small businesses when issuing contracts under DPA authorities. Section 701 of Title VII reiterates[104] and expands upon a requirement in Section 108 of Title I directing the President to "accord a strong preference for small business concerns which are subcontractors or suppliers, and, to the maximum extent practicable, to such small business concerns located in areas of high unemployment or areas that have demonstrated a continuing pattern of economic decline, as identified by the Secretary of Labor."[105] These provisions were not amended in the Reauthorization of 2009, nor did the delegation of the authority change in E.O. 13603.

Definitions of Key Terms in the DPA

The DPA statute historically has included a section of definitions.[106] Though *national defense* is perhaps the most important term, there are additional definitions provided both in current law and in E.O. 13603.[107] Over time, the list of definitions provided in both the law and implementing executive orders has been added to and edited, and the Reauthorization of 2009 was no exception.[108] Most notably, Congress added a definition for *homeland security* to place it within the context of *national defense*.[109] Likewise, in issuing E.O. 13603, supplementary definitions were amended, added, and removed definitions that had been listed in E.O. 12919, as amended.[110]

---

[104] 50 U.S.C. Appx. §2151; Section 701 of the DPA.

[105] 50 U.S.C. Appx. §2078; Section 108(a) of the DPA.

[106] The original law provided five definitions, including a definition of "national defense." See Section 702 of P.L. 81-774.

[107] In total, there are 17 terms defined in law in 50 U.S.C. Appx. §2152, and 13 additional definitions in Section 801 of E.O. 13603.

[108] 123 Stat 2017-2018. Congress amended, in addition to the definition of *national defense*, the existing definitions of *critical component, critical technology, domestic industrial base, industrial resources,* and *services.* Congress struck the definitions for *critical industry for national security, essential weapon system,* and *small business concern owned and controlled by socially and economically disadvantaged individuals.* Congress added the definitions *guaranteeing agency* and *homeland security.*

[109] 50 U.S.C. Appx. §2152(11). *Homeland security* means efforts "(A) to prevent terrorist attacks within the United States; (B) to reduce the vulnerability of the United States to terrorism; (C) to minimize damage from a terrorist attack in the United States; and (D) to recover from a terrorist attack in the United States."

[110] By comparison to Section 901 of E.O. 12919, as amended, Section 801 of E.O. 13603 altered the definitions *civil transportation, energy, food resources, food resource facilities, head of each agency engaged in procurement for the national defense, health resources,* and *water resources.* Section 801 of E.O. 13603 added the definitions *national defense* (same meaning as in statute), *offsets,* and *special priorities assistance.* It removed the definitions of *heads of other appropriate Federal departments and agencies,* and *metals and minerals.*

Industrial Base Assessments

To appropriately use numerous authorities of the DPA, especially Title III authorities, the President may require a detailed understanding of current domestic industrial capabilities and thereby need to obtain extensive information from private industries. Therefore, under Section 705 of the DPA, the President may "by regulation, subpoena, or otherwise obtain such information from ... any person as may be necessary or appropriate, in his discretion, to the enforcement or the administration of this Act [the DPA]."[111] This authority has been delegated to the Secretary of Commerce in E.O. 13603.[112] Though this authority has many potential implications and uses, it is most commonly associated with what the DOC's Bureau of Industry and Security calls "industrial base assessments."[113] These assessments are often conducted in coordination with the Departments of Defense and Homeland Security, as well as the private sector, to "monitor trends, benchmark industry performance, and raise awareness of diminishing manufacturing capabilities."[114] The statute includes a requirement that the President issue regulations to insure that the authority is used only after "the scope and purpose of the investigation, inspection, or inquiry to be made have been defined by competent authority, and it is assured that no adequate and authoritative data are available from any Federal or other responsible agency."[115] However, no such regulation has been issued by the executive branch.

Voluntary Agreements

Normally, voluntary agreements or plans of action between competing private industry interests could be subject to legal sanction under anti-trust statutes or contract law. Title VII of the DPA authorizes the President to "consult with representatives of industry, business, financing, agriculture, labor, and other interests in order to provide for the making by such persons, with the approval of the President, of voluntary agreements and plans of action to help provide for the national defense."[116] The President must determine that a "condition exists which may pose a direct threat to the national defense or its preparedness programs"[117] prior to engaging in the extensive consultation process. Following the consultation process, the President or appropriate delegate may approve and commence the agreement or plan of action.[118] Parties entering into such voluntary agreements are afforded a special legal defense if their actions within that agreement would otherwise violate antitrust or contract laws.[119]

- Historically, the National Infrastructure Advisory Council noted that the voluntary agreement authority has been used to "enable companies to cooperate

---

[111] 50 U.S.C. Appx. §2155(a); Section 705(a) of the DPA.

[112] Generally, see Section 104(d) of E.O. 13603.

[113] For examples of some publically available industrial base assessments, see the agency's website at http://www.bis.doc.gov/index.php/other-areas/office-of-technology-evaluation-ote/industrial-base-assessments.

[114] Ibid.

[115] 50 U.S.C. Appx. §2155(a); Section 705(a) of the DPA.

[116] 50 U.S.C. Appx. §2158(c)(1); Section 708(c)(1) of the DPA.

[117] Ibid. The consultation process is described in 50 U.S.C. Appx. §§2158(d) and (e); Section 708(d) and (e) of the DPA.

[118] 50 U.S.C. Appx. §2158(f); Section 708(f) of the DPA.

[119] 50 U.S.C. Appx. §2158, Section 708 of the DPA provides a legal defense to parties of voluntary agreements or plans of action that can be used in civil suits or criminal actions brought against them under anti-trust laws (§2158(j)) or for breach of contract (§2158(o)). These exemptions do not grant them blanket immunity from these laws.

in weapons manufacture, solving production problems and standardizing designs, specifications and processes," among other examples.[120] The Maritime Administration of the Department of Transportation manages the only currently established voluntary agreements in the federal government, the Voluntary Intermodal Sealift Agreement (commonly referred to as "VISA") and the Voluntary Tanker Agreement.[121] These agreements are established to ensure that the maritime industry can respond to the mobilization and transportation requirements of the Department of Defense.

- There were two substantive changes to this voluntary agreement authority in the Reauthorization of 2009.[122] First, in most circumstances, an individual with delegated authority must consult with the Attorney General or the Federal Trade Commission prior to finalizing the voluntary agreement. The revised statute now permits the finalization of a voluntary agreement without consultation with the Attorney General or Federal Trade Commission if the President determines, on a nondelegable basis, that it is needed to meet national defense requirements in the wake of a disaster that destroys or degrades critical infrastructure.[123] Second, the reauthorization extended the maximum term length for each voluntary agreement, once it is established, from two years to five years.[124]

The delegation of voluntary agreement authority did not change substantively with the issuance of E.O. 13603.[125] However, E.O. 13603 includes an explicit requirement that the Department of Homeland Security issue regulations on voluntary agreements in accordance with DPA statute.[126]

Nucleus Executive Reserve

In Title VII of the DPA, the President is authorized to establish a volunteer body of industry executives, the "Nucleus Executive Reserve," or more frequently called the National Defense Executive Reserve (NDER).[127] The NDER would be a pool of individuals with recognized expertise from various segments of the private sector and from government (except full-time federal employees). These individuals would be brought together for training in executive

---

[120] The National Infrastructure Advisory Council, *Framework for Dealing with Disasters and Related Interdependencies: Final Report and Recommendations*, Appendix G: The Defense Production Act, Washington, DC, July 14, 2009, p. 45, at http://www.dhs.gov/xlibrary/assets/niac/niac_framework_dealing_with_disasters.pdf.

[121] Department of Homeland Security, *The Defense Production Act Committee: Report to Congress*, August 2011, p. 10.

[122] 123 Stat. 2018-2019.

[123] See 123 Stat. 2018 and 50 U.S.C. Appx. §2158(c)(3); Section 708(c)(3) of the DPA. In a report released before the DPA reauthorization in 2009, the National Infrastructure Advisory Council (NIAC) suggested that the voluntary agreement authority could be especially useful for recovering privately owned critical infrastructure following a terrorist attack or natural disaster. However, NIAC was concerned that some of the restrictions for creating a voluntary agreement would unnecessarily delay using the authority following a major disaster. See The National Infrastructure Advisory Council, *Framework for Dealing with Disasters and Related Interdependencies: Final Report and Recommendations*, Appendix G: The Defense Production Act, Washington, DC, July 14, 2009, p. 48, at http://www.dhs.gov/xlibrary/assets/niac/niac_framework_dealing_with_disasters.pdf.

[124] 123 Stat. 2018. See 50 U.S.C. Appx. §2158(e)(2); Section 708(e)(2) of the DPA.

[125] Section 401 of E.O. 13603.

[126] The legal requirement for the regulations can be found at 50 U.S.C. Appx. §2158(e). FEMA's regulations can be found at 44 C.F.R. Part 332.

[127] 50 U.S.C. Appx. §2160(e); Section 710(e) of the DPA.

positions within the federal government in the event of an emergency that requires their employment. The historic concept of the NDER has been used as a means of improving the war mobilization and productivity of industries.[128] The Reauthorization of 2009 amended the statute by removing a clause that allowed the President to grant some exemptions to criminal statutes to NDER participants.[129]

The head of any governmental department or agency may establish a unit of the NDER and train its members.[130] No NDER unit is currently active, though the statute and E.O. 13603 still provide for this possibility. Units may be activated only when the Secretary of Homeland Security declares in writing that "an emergency affecting the national defense exists and that the activation of the unit is necessary to carry out the emergency program functions of the agency."[131]

Authorization of Appropriations

Appropriations for the purpose of the DPA are authorized by Section 711 of Title VII.[132] The only regular annual appropriation for the purposes of the DPA is made in the Department of Defense appropriations bill to the DPA Fund, though appropriations could be made in other bills.[133] Prior to the Reauthorization of 2009, Section 711 contained a separate provision authorizing appropriations within a defined time period for Title III specifically.[134] However, this separate provision was removed in 2009. Arguably, this separate authorization was redundant with the overall authorization of appropriation.

Committee on Foreign Investment in the United States

Another section of Title VII grants the President authority to review certain corporate mergers, acquisitions, and takeovers, and to investigate the potential impact on national security of such actions.[135] The statute empowers the President to suspend these actions for any period he considers appropriate, or to prohibit transactions found to threaten impairment of national security. This is the so-called Exon-Florio Amendment, which designated a pre-existing interagency body, the Committee on Foreign Investment in the United States (CFIUS) chaired by

---

[128] President Dwight D. Eisenhower created the NDER in 1956 by issuing E.O.10660 under the authorities granted in Title VII. It has served as a vehicle for training highly qualified private industry executives in war production mobilization should the nation be faced with the need to place the nation's industrial base on a war footing. This program was inspired by the experiences of the War Industries Board of World War I and the War Production Board of World War II, when corporate executives were brought into government service, often with little or no compensation, to organize the nation's industries for war production. For background on the origins and operation of the War Industries Board, see Paul A. C. Koistinen, "The 'Industrial-Military Complex' in Historical Perspective: World War I," *The Business History Review*, Vol. 41, No. 4 (Winter, 1967), pp. 378-403; and Robert D. Cuff, "A 'Dollar-a-Year Man' in Government: George N. Peek and the War Industries Board," *The Business History Review*, vol. 41, no. 4 (Winter, 1967), pp. 404-420.

[129] 123 Stat 2019.

[130] Section 501(c) in E.O. 13603.

[131] Section 501(e) in E.O. 13603.

[132] 50 U.S.C. Appx §2161

[133] See **Table 1** above for a list of recent appropriations.

[134] See the former 50 U.S.C. Appx §2161(b) [2006 Edition], what was Section 711(b) of the DPA.

[135] 50 U.S.C. Appx §2170; Section 721 of the DPA.

---

the Secretary of the Treasury, as the entity through which the President acts.[136] For example, CFIUS reviews resulted in President George H. W. Bush ordering the China National Aero-Technology Import & Export Corporation to divest itself of Seattle-based MAMCO Manufacturing in 1990 and in the approval by President George W. Bush of the acquisition of IBM's personal computer and laptop division by Chinese-owned Lenovo in 2005. Various CFIUS authorities are delegated by the President in E.O. 11858, *Foreign Investment in the United States*, originally issued in 1975, not in E.O. 13603.[137] The Reauthorization of 2009 did not amend this authority.

Defense Production Act Committee

The Defense Production Act Committee (DPAC) is an interagency body established by the 2009 reauthorization of the DPA.[138] The DPAC was created to advise the President regarding the effective use of DPA authorities. Comments made by Representative Melvin Watt during floor consideration of the 2009 bill suggest that part of the legislative intent in creating the DPAC may have been to elevate the policy discussions on the DPA to a Cabinet-level body.[139] Congress exempted the DPAC from the requirements of the Federal Advisory Committee Act.[140]

The statute assigns membership in the DPAC to the head of each federal agency delegated DPA authorities, as well as the Chairperson of the Council of Economic Advisors. A full list of the members of the DPAC is included in E.O. 13603.[141] The DPA also requires the President to designate one of the members as Chairperson of the DPAC. President Obama has appointed the Secretaries of Homeland Security and Defense to serve as the Chairperson on an annually rotating basis.[142] The President is also required to appoint an Executive Director to the DPAC to support the Chairperson as needed. The current Executive Director is the Deputy Assistant Secretary of Defense for Manufacturing and Industrial Base Policy. The only statutory responsibility of the DPAC is to provide an annual report that reviews the current use of DPA authorities, and provides recommendations for improving DPA implementation in the government or for amending DPA statute.[143] This report is provided to the Senate Committee on Banking, Housing, and Urban Affairs and the House Committee on Financial Services. The first annual DPAC report, for the calendar year 2010, was submitted in August of 2011. The reports for calendar years 2011 and

---

[136] For more on CFIUS, see CRS Report RL33388, *The Committee on Foreign Investment in the United States (CFIUS)*, by James K. Jackson.

[137] See Executive Order 11858, "Foreign Investment in the United States," 40 *Federal Register* 20263, May 7, 1975.

[138] See 123 Stat. 2019-2020 for the creation of the DPAC in statute. The DPAC is now authorized in Section 722 of the DPA, 50 U.S.C. Appx. §2171. The DPAC website is at http://www.acq.osd mil/mibp/dpac.html.

[139] Rep. Melvin Watt, "Defense Production Act Reauthorization of 2009," House consideration of S. 1677, *Congressional Record*, September 23, 2009, pp. H9817-H9818; and Sen. Christopher Dodd, "Defense Production Act Reauthorization of 2009," Senate consideration of S. 1677, *Congressional Record*, September 16, 2009, p. S9480.

[140] 50 U.S.C. Appx. §2171(e); Section 722(e) of the DPA. For more on the Federal Advisory Committee Act, see CRS Report R40520, *Federal Advisory Committees: An Overview*, by Wendy Ginsberg.

[141] Section 701 of E.O. 13603.

[142] Presidential Documents, "Designating the Chairperson of the Defense Production Act," 75 *Federal Register* 32087, June 7, 2010. This relationship between the Secretaries of Homeland Security and Defense is supported by a memorandum of agreement, available at http://www.acq.osd mil/mibp/resources html. The Secretary of Homeland Security served as the first Chairperson, from April 1, 2010, to March 31, 2011; the Secretary of Defense then served from April 1, 2011 to March 31, 2012, and so forth.

[143] 50 U.S.C. Appx. §2171(d); Section 722(d) of the DPA.

2012 were combined and submitted to Congress on March 31, 2013. As of January 31, 2014, a DPAC report for the calendar year 2013 was not available to CRS.

Impact of Offsets Report

Offsets are industrial compensation practices that foreign governments or companies require of U.S. firms as a condition of purchase in either government-to-government or commercial sales of defense articles and/or defense services as defined by the Arms Export Control Act (22 U.S.C. §2751, et seq.) and the International Traffic in Arms Regulations (22 C.F.R. §§120-130). In defense trade, such industrial compensation can include mandatory co-production, licensed production, subcontractor production, technology transfer, and foreign investment.

The Secretary of Commerce is required to prepare and to transmit to the appropriate congressional committees an annual report on the impact of offsets on defense preparedness, industrial competitiveness, employment, and trade. Specifically, the report discusses "offsets" in the government or commercial sales of defense materials.[144] The Reauthorization of 2009 moved this reporting provision to Title VII from Title III.[145] The reporting provision did not change substantively in the move to Title VII.

Issues for Congress

Reauthorization of the DPA in the 113th Congress

All DPA authorities in Titles I, III, and VII are scheduled to terminate on September 30, 2014, with the exception of four sections.[146] As explained in Section 717 of the DPA, the sections that are exempt from termination are:

- 50 U.S.C. Appx. §2074, Section 104 of the DPA that prohibits both the imposition of wage or price controls without prior congressional authorization and the mandatory compliance of any private person to assist in the production of chemical or biological warfare capabilities;

- 50 U.S.C. Appx. §2157, Section 707 of the DPA that grants persons limited immunity from liability for complying with DPA-authorized regulations;

- 50 U.S.C. Appx. §2158, Section 708 of the DPA that provides for the establishment of voluntary agreements; and

- 50 U.S.C. Appx. §2170, Section 721 of the DPA, the so-called Exon-Florio Amendment, that gives the President and CFIUS review authority over certain corporate acquisition activities.

---

[144] Offsets are defined in Section 801(k) of E.O. 13603. Offsets can be direct, where offsetting sales of goods and services are related to the military export sale being contracted, or indirect, where they are not. This report is prepared by the Department of Commerce Bureau of Industry and Security (BIS) and is posted online at http://www.bis.doc.gov/defenseindustrialbaseprograms/osies/offsets/default.htm.

[145] 123 Stat. 2020. The reporting requirement moved to Section 723 from Section 309 of the DPA; to the current 50 U.S.C. Appx. §2171 from the former 50 U.S.C. Appx. §2099 [2006 Edition].

[146] 123 Stat. 2006; 50 U.S.C. Appx. §2166.

In addition, Section 717(c) provides that any termination of sections of the DPA "shall not affect the disbursement of funds under, or the carrying out of, any contract, guarantee, commitment or other obligation entered into pursuant to this Act" prior to its termination. This means, for instance, that prioritized contracts or Section 303 projects created with DPA authorities prior to September 30, 2014, would still be executed until completion even if the DPA is not reauthorized. Similarly, the statute specifies that the authority to investigate, subpoena, and otherwise collect information necessary to administer the provisions of the act, as provided by Section 705 of the DPA, will not expire until two years after the termination of the DPA.[147]

Frequently, Congress has elected to reauthorize the DPA by extending the termination date provided in Section 717 for a limited period, such as a year, without making significant amendments to the overall statute.[148] In other circumstances, Congress has reauthorized the law by extending the Section 717 date for several years while also amending the other provisions of the law.[149] In either circumstance, reauthorizations have typically been presented as discrete bills, though on occasion the DPA has been reauthorized through a provision in a larger legislative vehicle such as the National Defense Authorization Act.[150] For a chronology of all laws reauthorizing the DPA since inception, see **Table A-4**.

H.R. 4809

H.R. 4809 passed the House under suspension of the rules on July 29, 2014. If enacted, Section 1 of the bill would reauthorize the expiring provisions of the DPA for five years, from September 30, 2014, to September 30, 2019. The remaining sections of the bill would reform existing provisions of the DPA.

Section 2 of the bill would make several revisions to the Defense Production Act Committee (DPAC), which was established in the Reauthorization of 2009 and is currently authorized in Section 722 of the DPA. First, Section 2 would restate the general purpose of the DPAC. Originally, the committee was created to advise the President on the effective use of the full scope of authorities of the act. The bill would instead redirect this to coordination and planning for the use of Title I priorities and allocations authority within the executive branch.[151] Notably, this proposed change would likely result in the abolishment of several "industrial capability assessment study groups" created under DPAC authority.[152] Second, Section 2 would supersede the rotating chair system for the DPAC, which was established by presidential memorandum. Under the existing procedure, the Secretary of Defense and Secretary of Homeland Security rotate annually in the DPAC chair.[153] Instead, the bill would direct the President to appoint as chair the "head of the agency to which the President has delegated primary responsibility for government-wide coordination of the authorities in this Act." As currently established in E.O.

---

[147] 50 U.S.C. Appx. §2155(a); Section 705(a) of the DPA. Thus, under current law, Section 705 authority would expire on September 30, 2016.

[148] For examples, see P.L. 110-367, P.L. 106-363, or P.L. 102-193.

[149] For examples, see P.L. 111-67, P.L. 108-195, or P.L. 102-558.

[150] For example, the DPA was reauthorized for a year by a provision in Section 1072 of P.L. 105-261, the Strom Thurmond National Defense Authorization Act for Fiscal Year 1999.

[151] For more on the DPAC, see the section entitled "Defense Production Act Committee" of the report.

[152] For more on these study groups, see the DPAC website at http://www.acq.osd mil/mibp/dpac.html.

[153] See Presidential Documents, "Designating the Chairperson of the Defense Production Act," 75 *Federal Register* 32087, June 7, 2010.

13603 delegations, the Secretary of Homeland Security appears to be the most likely chair-designate, but the language of the proposed bill could allow the President to appoint another Secretary.[154] Third, Section 2 of the bill would require the chair to appoint a person to coordinate all committee activities. Finally, Section 2 of the bill would revise the annual reporting requirements of the DPAC to emphasize Title I priority and allocation authority and to require the report to include updated copies of Title I-related rules.

Section 3 of the bill accentuates the Title I rulemaking requirement first directed in the Reauthorization of 2009 by requiring delegated agencies with Title I authority to issue and annually review their final rules. Of the six departments to which the President delegated Title I authority, only three (Commerce, Energy, and Transportation) had issued final rules as of June 10, 2014. The Departments of Agriculture, Defense, and Health and Human Services have not yet completed final rules.[155]

Section 4 of the bill would revise the Title III, Section 303 authority of the DPA.[156] First, Section 4(a) of the bill would require the President, on a non-delegable basis, to provide written explanatory materials on how actions taken under Section 303 would meet several presidential determinations required by law (that the actions are essential to the national defense and that sufficient commercial production and supply of the good would otherwise not be available). Current law allows these determinations to be delegated beyond the President. In recent practice, the Under Secretary of Defense for Acquisition, Technology, and Logistics has been responsible for making these determinations and for submitting signed explanatory materials to the committees of jurisdiction.[157] Section 4(a) would also reinstitute two provisions, with minor revisions, that were removed from the law in the Reauthorization of 2009. In addition to the existing conditions in Section 303(a)(5) of the DPA that must be determined to be met before using Section 303 authorities, the President would be required to determine that the actions taken are "the most cost effective, expedient, and practical alternative method for meeting the need."[158]

Further, Section 4(a) of the bill would reinstitute another deleted provision. That provision required that, should the aggregate cost of planned actions taken to address an industrial base

---

[154] See Section 104(b)(2) of E.O. 13603, which includes as one of the responsibilities of the Secretary of Homeland Security to "provide for the central coordination of the plans and programs incident to authorities and functions delegated under this order ... "

[155] For more on this rulemaking requirement, see the section entitled "How Priorities and Allocations Changed in the Reauthorization of 2009 and E.O. 13603" of the report. The Department of Agriculture has a proposed rulemaking that has not been finalized, see Department of Agriculture, "Agriculture Priorities and Allocations System," 76 *Federal Register* 29084, May 19, 2011. The Department of Energy issued a final rule codified in 10 C.F.R. Part 217, see Department of Energy, "Energy Priorities and Allocations System Regulations," 75 *Federal Register* 41405, July 16, 2010. The Department of Transportation issued a final rule codified in 49 C.F.R. Part 33, see Department of Transportation, "Prioritization and Allocation Authority Exercised by the Secretary of Transportation Under the Defense Production Act," 77 *Federal Register* 59793, October 1, 2012. The Administration has reported that new rules are being prepared by the Department of Agriculture and the Department of Health and Human Services, but did not mention the development of a rule by the Department of Defense. See Department of Homeland Security, *The Defense Production Act Committee: Report to Congress*, March 31, 2013, p. 4.

[156] For more on this authority, see the section entitled "Purchase, Purchase Commitments, and Installation of Equipment" of the report.

[157] The Under Secretary of Defense for Acquisition, Technology, and Logistics is delegated this responsibility by the Secretary of Defense in DOD Directive 4400.01E, Defense Production Act Programs, September 14, 2007, at http://www.dtic.mil/whs/directives/corres/pdf/440001p.pdf.

[158] This requirement previously existed in law at Section 303(a)(5)(C) of the DPA, the former 50 U.S.C. Appx. §2093(a)(5)(C) [2006 edition].

shortfall under Section 303 exceed $50 million, those actions must first be authorized by an act of Congress. This monetary limitation on action was removed from law in the Reauthorization of 2009 and replaced with a general notification to the committees of jurisdiction for projects estimated to cost more than $50 million.[159] The proposed revision would require the President to both notify the committees of jurisdiction and obtain authorization in an act of Congress before taking actions in excess of $50 million to address a manufacturing capacity or supply shortfall.

Section 4(b) of the bill would retroactively exempt any existing Title III project (i.e., one that has already been determined to meet requirements of the law) from the requirements of the proposed Section 4(a). In other words, if actions to address a shortfall for any existing project do not exceed $50 million currently, but ultimately do so in the future, that project would not require direct authorization from Congress.

In their totality, the revisions made by Section 4 of the bill, if enacted, may partially limit exiting Section 303 authority. For example, if the bill is enacted as currently written, Congress would be able to refuse authorization to new Title III projects and actions that would push the aggregate cost above the $50 million threshold. However, the President would retain the ability to waive these requirements in periods of national emergency or if the actions are necessary to avert a shortfall that would severely impair national defense capability.[160]

Section 5 of the bill would revise the existing "such sums as necessary" authorization of appropriations found in Section 711 of Title VII of the DPA.[161] Instead, the bill would authorize the appropriation of $133 million per fiscal year, starting in FY2015, to carry out the provisions and purposes of the Defense Production Act. Past appropriations to the DPA Fund are listed in **Table 1**, which shows that the annual average direct appropriation to the DPA Fund between FY2010 and FY2014 was $127.7 million,[162] with a high of $223.5 million in FY2013 and a low of $34.3 million in FY2011. Monies in the DPA Fund are available until expended, so annual appropriations may carry over from year to year if not expended.

Considerations for Amending the Defense Production Act of 1950

In conjunction with or separate from a reauthorization bill, Congress could amend the DPA in order to extend, expand, restrict, or otherwise clarify the powers granted to the President in the DPA. For example, Congress could eliminate certain authorities altogether, such as the Section 710(e) authority underpinning the National Defense Executive Reserve. Likewise, Congress could expand the DPA to include new authorities to address novel threats to the national

---

[159] This limitation previously existed in law at Section 303(a)(6)(C) of the DPA, the former 50 U.S.C. Appx. §2093(a)(6)(C) [2006 edition]. Generally, few Title III projects exceed the $50 million threshold, and current projects average about $20.7 million per contract. An example of a past authorization made by Congress for Title III actions exceeding $50 million, to correct a shortfall for high-purity beryllium metal, can be found in §842 of P.L. 111-84, the National Defense Authorization Act for Fiscal Year 2010, 123 Stat. 2418.

[160] See §303(a)(7) of the DPA, 50 U.S.C. Appx. §2093(a)(7).

[161] 50 U.S.C. Appx §2161.

[162] This average figure increases by $9 million to $136.72 if one includes the $45 million authorized transfer from the overall appropriation of $1,912 million for the Department of Energy's Energy Efficiency and Renewable Energy account in FY2014.

defense.[163] In addition to addressing the specific authorities granted in Title I, Title III, and Title VII of the DPA, Congress may also consider other amendments to the DPA.

Declaration of Policy

The "Declaration of Policy" in the DPA describes the general intentions of the authorities it confers to the President. One option for Congress is to amend this section of the statute in order to expand, restrict, or clarify the overall purpose of the authorities. For instance, Congress could include further discussion on the specific circumstances under which it finds DPA authorities are appropriate for use by the President. Though this section serves as a guide for the overall use of DPA authorities, changes to the Declaration of Policy may not fully endow or deny the President's authorities covered in the titles of the DPA without also amending the DPA's other provisions.

Rather than passing legislation to amend the text of the DPA, Congress could adopt a resolution clarifying the purpose of the DPA authorities. For example, one such resolution introduced in the 112th Congress, H.Con.Res. 110, states that is it the "Sense of Congress" that the DPA should not be used to "confiscate personal or private property, to force conscription into the Armed Forces on the American people, to force civilians to engage in labor against their will or without compensation, or to force private businesses to relinquish goods or services without compensation." However, "Sense of Congress" resolutions of this nature do not carry the force of law.[164]

Definitions

Congress may wish to amend the definitions of key terms found in the DPA to shape the scope and use of the authorities, especially the definition of *national defense*. As an example, Congress could amend the definition of national defense to remove *space* from the definition, and as a result the President may be less able to use DPA authorities to support space-related projects.[165] On the other hand, for example, Congress could amend the definition of *national defense* to specifically include counter-narcotics, cybersecurity, or organized crime. Doing so would more explicitly enable the use of DPA authorities to address these homeland security and national defense concerns.

Appropriations to the DPA Fund

Congress could increase or reduce future appropriations to the DPA Fund to manage the scope of Title III projects initiated by the President (see **Table 1** for appropriations to the DPA Fund since

---

[163] For example, Congress may consider creating new authorities to address specific concerns relating to production and security of cyber-related infrastructure and assets necessary for the national defense. The Homeland Security Studies and Analysis Institute has suggested that DPA authorities, especially Section 303 authorities, might be helpful in addressing cybersecurity threats, though the legality of such action remains unknown. See Homeland Security Studies and Analysis Institute, *An Analysis of the Primary Authorities Supporting and Governing the Efforts of the Department of Homeland Security to Secure the Cyberspace of the United States*, Arlington, VA, May 24, 2011, p. 28, at http://www.homelandsecurity.org/docs/reports/MHF-and-EG-Analysis-of-authorities-supporting-efforts-of-DHS-to-secure-cyberspace-2011.pdf.

[164] For more on this issue, see CRS Report 98-825, *"Sense of" Resolutions and Provisions*, by Christopher M. Davis.

[165] For the definition of national defense, see 50 U.S.C. Appx. §2152(14); Section 702(14) of the DPA.

FY2010). Use of the DPA Fund, however, is specific to Title III. Therefore, adjusting appropriations to the DPA Fund is unlikely to have an effect on the President's ability to exercise his authorities under the other titles of the DPA, unless Congress writes specific language in the appropriations statute changing the nature of the Fund itself or authorizing its used beyond a specific title. Within the scope of a reauthorization bill, Congress may wish to reintroduce of a separate provision in Section 711 of the DPA authorizing only certain appropriation amounts over a given time period for Title III or other DPA authorities.[166] Likewise, Congress may wish to direct the usage of such funds more specifically, such as has been done recently in relation to advanced drop-in biofuels.[167]

Considerations for Oversight of Ongoing DPA Activities

Expand Reporting or Notification Requirements

Congress might be satisfied with the existing scope and use of DPA authorities by the President, but may wish to add more extensive notification and reporting requirements on the use of all or specific authorities in the DPA. Additional reporting or notification requirements could involve formal notification of Congress prior to or after the use of certain authorities in certain circumstances. For example, Congress may wish for the President to notify Congress (or the committees of jurisdiction) when the priorities and allocations authority is used on a contract over a certain dollar amount. Congress might also consider expanding the existing reporting requirements of Defense Production Act Committee (DPAC), to include semi-annual updates on the recent use of authorities or explanations about controversial determinations. Thus far, the DPAC has failed to regularly submit an annual report on time to the committees of jurisdiction, which may be limiting the ability of Congress to oversee the use of the DPA.

Existing requirements could also be expanded from notifying/reporting to the committees of jurisdiction to the Congress as a whole, or to include other interested committees, such as the House and Senate Armed Services Committees. Additionally, Congress may consider reestablishing a select committee with a similar purpose as the Joint Committee on Defense Production that was repealed in 1992 by Congress.[168]

Rulemaking Requirements

In the Reauthorization of 2009, Congress required agencies with delegated priorities and allocations authority under Title I of the DPA to issue final rules creating standards and procedures for the use of the authority. Similarly, a rulemaking requirement exists for the voluntary agreement authority in Title VII.[169] Congress may wish to review the compliance with these existing rulemaking requirements, and potentially expand them for other authorities included in the DPA. For example, Congress may consider whether the President should

---

[166] For example, appropriations for Title I could be authorized for only one year, but for Title III for five, and vice versa. See the "Authorization of Appropriations" section of this report for more.

[167] Section 315, P.L. 112-239, National Defense Authorization Act for Fiscal Year 2013. For more on this topic, see CRS Report R42859, *DOD Alternative Fuels: Policy, Initiatives and Legislative Activity.*

[168] P.L. 102-558, 106 Stat. 4219. This committee was intended to review the programs established by the DPA, and advise the standing committees in their legislation on the subject.

[169] 50 U.S.C. Appx. §2158(e); Section 708(e) of the DPA. This rule is established in 44 C.F.R. Part 332.

promulgate rules establishing standards and procedures for the use of all or certain Title III authorities.

Amend Authority Delegations

Congress may consider limiting the use of certain DPA authorities to specific departments and agencies. To do so, Congress could amend the President's delegation of DPA authorities, superseding those made in E.O. 13603, by amending the statute to assign specific authorities to individual Cabinet Secretaries as opposed to the President. Further, Congress could expand the use of the legislative clause "on a nondelegable basis" to ensure that the authority is not delegated beyond the person identified in the statute.[170] In considering these options, Congress may determine that the use of some authorities by certain agencies is appropriate and necessary for the national defense, but not for others.

---

[170] For an example of this clause, see 50 U.S.C. Appx. §2158(c)(3); Section 708(c)(3) of the DPA.

Appendix. Additional Resources and Summary Tables

There are many government-sponsored websites, reports, and guides that discuss various aspects of the Defense Production Act in depth that may be of interest to Congress. **Table A-1** provides a list of some of these resources.

Table A-1. Additional Resources by Defense Production Act Subject

DPA Subject	Additional Resources
General Information on DPA Authorities	DPAC website at http://www.acq.osd.mil/mibp/dpac.html.
	FEMA website on the DPA at http://www.fema.gov/defense-production-act-program-division.
	U.S. Government Accountability Office, *Defense Production Act: Agencies Lack Policies and Guidance for Use of Key Authorities*, GAO-08-854, June 2008, at http://www.gao.gov/products/GAO-08-854.
	The National Infrastructure Advisory Council, *Framework for Dealing with Disasters and Related Interdependencies: Final Report and Recommendations*, Appendix G: The Defense Production Act, Washington, D.C., July 14, 2009, pp. 40-49, at http://www.dhs.gov/xlibrary/assets/niac/niac_framework_dealing_with_disasters.pdf.
Title I: Priorities and Allocations	Department of Commerce "Defense Priorities and Allocations System" website at http://www.bis.doc.gov/dpas/default.htm.
	Department of Defense, *Priorities and Allocations Manual*, 4400.1-M, Washington, D.C., February 21, 2002, at http://www.acq.osd.mil/mibp/docs/44001m.pdf.
Title III: Authorities and Projects	Website with listing and description of Title III projects at http://www.dpatitle3.com/dpa_db/.
	A 2012 brochure produced by the Department of Defense on Title III projects at http://dpatitle3.com/Title_III%202012%20Brochure.pdf.
Committee on Foreign Investment in the United States (CFIUS)	Department of Treasury CFIUS website at http://www.treasury.gov/resource-center/international/Pages/Committee-on-Foreign-Investment-in-US.aspx.
	CRS Report RL33388, *The Committee on Foreign Investment in the United States (CFIUS)*, by James K. Jackson.
Impact of Offsets in Defense Trade	Department of Commerce website on offsets at http://www.bis.doc.gov/defenseindustrialbaseprograms/osies/offsets/default.htm.

Source: CRS.

Table A-2. Substantive Provisions of the Defense Production Act, Related Portions of Executive Order 13603, and Associated Regulations

Authority and DPA Statute	Related Portions of Executive Order 13603[a]	Regulations or Guiding Documents	Summary of How the Authority Changed in the Reauthorization of 2009	Example of Use of Authority
Declaration of Policy; Section 2 of the DPA, 50 U.S.C. Appx. §2062	Sections 101, 102, and 103	Not applicable	Expanded the "Statement of Policy" to specifically advocate the use of the DPA in domestic preparedness and responses to terrorist attacks and natural hazards.	Not applicable
Priorities and Allocations; Title I of the DPA, 50 U.S.C. Appx. §2071	Part II	10 C.F.R. Part 217, 15 C.F.R. Part 700 and 49 C.F.R. Part 33. More regulations are being proposed under the Reauthorization of 2009.[b]	Required a rulemaking by all federal departments and agencies delegated Title I authorities within 270 days of enactment.	Priority contracts have been issued to support the Integrated Ballistic Missile Defense System.[c]
Loan Guarantees; Section 301 and 302 of Title III of the DPA, 50 U.S.C. Appx. §§2091 and 2092	Part III	Not applicable	Updated authorities to comply with the Federal Credit Reform Act by mandating that loans and loan guarantees are appropriated by Congress before issuance. Amended the factors for determining if a guarantee or loan is needed for national defense. Limited the authority of the President to waive requirements on how the guarantees and loans can be used and issued.	According to the DPAC, none in recent history.
Purchases, Purchase Commitments, and Installation of Equipment; Section 303 of Title III of the DPA, 50 U.S.C. Appx. §2093	Part III	Not applicable	Expanded some Section 303 authorities and amended the notification and determination requirements prior to use of authorities.	"Lithium Ion Space Battery Production Initiative," which involved remodeling a facility and the purchase and installation of equipment to create "a viable domestic source of spacecraft-quality rechargeable Lithium Ion (Li Ion) cells and the critical materials required to produce these cells."[d]

Authority and DPA Statute	Related Portions of Executive Order 13603[a]	Regulations or Guiding Documents	Summary of How the Authority Changed in the Reauthorization of 2009	Example of Use of Authority
Definitions; Section 702 of the DPA, 50 U.S.C. Appx. §2152	Section 802	Not applicable	Amended the definitions: "national defense," "critical component," "critical technology," "domestic industrial base," "industrial resources," and "services."	Not applicable
			Revoked the definitions "critical industry for national security," "essential weapon system," and "small business concern owned and controlled by socially and economically disadvantaged individuals."	
			Added the definitions "guaranteeing agency" and "homeland security."	
Voluntary Agreements; Section 708 of the DPA, 50 U.S.C. Appx. §2158	Part IV	44 C.F.R. Part 332	Created an exemption from some prerequisites to establish a voluntary agreement when the President determines a voluntary agreement is needed to meet national defense requirements following a disaster that destroys or degrades critical infrastructure.[e]	Voluntary Intermodal Sealift Agreement (VISA) managed by the Maritime Administration in the U.S. Department of Transportation.[f]
			Extended the term of voluntary agreements from 2 to 5 years before they need to be renewed.	
National Defense Executive Reserve (NDER): Section 710 of the DPA, 50 U.S.C. Appx. §2160	Part V	Interim Guidance for the NDER Program[g]	Removed a provision that allowed the President to grant some exemptions to criminal statutes to participants in the NDER.	Not applicable
Committee on Foreign Investment in the United States (CFIUS): Section 721 of the DPA, 50 U.S.C. Appx. §2170	Executive Order 11858: Foreign Investment in the United States, as amended.	31 C.F.R. Part 800, as amended	No changes were made.	See CRS Report RL33388, *The Committee on Foreign Investment in the United States (CFIUS)*, by James K. Jackson.

Authority and DPA Statute	Related Portions of Executive Order 13603[a]	Regulations or Guiding Documents	Summary of How the Authority Changed in the Reauthorization of 2009	Example of Use of Authority
Defense Production Act Committee (DPAC); Section 722 of the DPA, 50 U.S.C. Appx. §2171	Part VII	Presidential Memorandum Designating the Chairperson of the Committee; Charter of the DPAC; MOU between DHS and DoD on their shared responsibilities to support the DPAC.[h]	The DPAC is a new federal government interagency body established by the Reauthorization of 2009.	The DPAC has established four different "study groups" to assess industrial capabilities necessary for the national defense, and another study group to develop recommendations for improving the DPA via legislation or regulation.[i]

Source: CRS analysis of E.O. 13603 and 50 U.S.C. Appx. §2061 et seq. and information from available resources.

Notes:

a. Unless otherwise noted, provisions cited are found in E.O. 13603.

b. See footnote 46 for additional information.

c. For more examples, see Department of Homeland Security, *The Defense Production Act Committee: Report to Congress*, Washington, DC, August 2011, p. 8.

d. See specifically http://www.dpatitle3.com/dpa_db/project.php?id=67. For a current list of all DPA Title III projects, see http://www.dpatitle3.com/dpa_db/.

e. 50 U.S.C. Appx. §2158(c)(3); Section 708(c)(3) of the DPA.

f. For more, see approval of the VISA program in the *Federal Register* at Maritime Administration, "Voluntary Intermodal Sealift Agreement," 75 *Federal Register* 14245, March 24, 2010. See also http://www.marad.dot.gov/ships_shipping_landing_page/national_security/vol_intermodal_sealift_agreement/vol_intermodal_sealift_agreement.htm.

g. Federal Emergency Management Agency, *The National Defense Executive Reserve: Policies and Procedures Manual*, Washington, DC, June 20, 2007, at http://www.fema.gov/library/viewRecord.do?id=3606.

h. These documents are available for download at http://www.acq.osd.mil/mibp/resources.html.

i. See http://www.acq.osd.mil/mibp/dpac.html. Part of the policy of the United States, as provided in Section 2(b)(1) of the DPA, is to "continuously assess the capability of the domestic industrial base to satisfy production requirements under both peacetime and emergency conditions, specifically evaluating the availability of adequate production sources, including subcontractors and suppliers, materials, skilled labor, and professional and technical personnel."

Table A-3. Delegation of Priorities and Allocations Authorities to Cabinet Secretaries

Cabinet Secretary	Delegated Area of Authority in E.O. 13603[a]	Definitions in E.O. 13603[b]
Secretary of Agriculture	Food resources, food resource facilities, livestock resources, veterinary resources, plant health resources, and the domestic distribution of farm equipment and commercial fertilizer	"Farm equipment" means equipment, machinery, and repair parts manufactured for use on farms in connection with the production or preparation for market use of food resources.
		"Fertilizer" means any product or combination of products that contain one or more of the elements nitrogen, phosphorus, and potassium for use as a plant nutrient.
		"Food resources" means all commodities and products (simple, mixed, or compound), or complements to such commodities or products, that are capable of being ingested by either human beings or animals, irrespective of other uses to which such commodities or products may be put, at all stages of processing from the raw commodity to the products thereof in vendible form for human or animal consumption. "Food resources" also means potable water packaged in commercially marketable containers, all starches, sugars, vegetable and animal or marine fats and oils, seed, cotton, hemp, and flax fiber, but does not mean any such material after it loses its identity as an agricultural commodity or agricultural product.
		"Food resource facilities" means plants, machinery, vehicles (including on farm), and other facilities required for the production, processing, distribution, and storage (including cold storage) of food resources, and for the domestic distribution of farm equipment and fertilizer (excluding transportation thereof).
Secretary of Energy	All forms of energy	"Energy" means all forms of energy including petroleum, gas (both natural and manufactured), electricity, solid fuels (including all forms of coal, coke, coal chemicals, coal liquefaction, and coal gasification), solar, wind, other types of renewable energy, atomic energy, and the production, conservation, use, control, and distribution (including pipelines) of all of these forms of energy.
Secretary of Health and Human Services	Health resources	"Health resources" means drugs, biological products, medical devices, materials, facilities, health supplies, services and equipment required to diagnose, mitigate or prevent the impairment of, improve, treat, cure, or restore the physical or mental health conditions of the population.
Secretary of Transportation	All forms of civil transportation	"Civil transportation" includes movement of persons and property by all modes of transportation in interstate, intrastate, or foreign commerce within the United States, its territories and possessions, and the District of Columbia, and related public storage and warehousing, ports, services, equipment and facilities, such as transportation carrier shop and repair facilities. "Civil transportation" also shall include direction, control, and coordination of civil transportation capacity regardless of ownership. "Civil transportation" shall not include transportation owned or controlled by the Department of Defense, use of petroleum and gas pipelines, and coal slurry pipelines used only to supply energy production facilities directly.
Secretary of Defense	Water resources	"Water resources" means all usable water, from all sources, within the jurisdiction of the United States, that can be managed, controlled, and allocated to meet emergency requirements, except "water resources" does not include usable water that qualifies as "food resources."

Cabinet Secretary	Delegated Area of Authority in E.O. 13603[a]	Definitions in E.O. 13603[b]
Secretary of Commerce	All other materials, services, and facilities, including construction materials	Materials, services, and facilities are all defined in statute; see 50 U.S.C. Appx. §§2152(13), (16), and (8), respectively.

Source: CRS analysis of E.O. 13603 and 50 U.S.C. Appx. §§2061 et seq.

Notes:

a. See Section 201(a)(1) to (6) of E.O. 13603.

b. These definitions are found in Section 802 of E.O. 13603.

Table A-4. Chronology of Laws Reauthorizing the Defense Production Act of 1950

Public Law and Statutes at Large Citation, and Date of Approval	General Expiration Date[a]
P.L. 81-774, 64 Stat. 798, September 8, 1950	June 30, 1951
P.L. 82-69, 65 Stat. 110, June 30, 1951	July 31, 1951
P.L. 82-96, 65 Stat. 131, July 31 1951	June 30, 1952
P.L. 82-429, 66 Stat. 296, June 30, 1952	June 30, 1953
P.L. 83-95, 67 Stat. 129, June 30, 1953[b]	June 30, 1955[b]
P.L. 84-119, 69 Stat. 225, June 30, 1955	July 31, 1955
P.L. 84-295, 69 Stat. 580, August 9, 1955	June 30, 1956
P.L. 84-632, 70 Stat. 408, June 29, 1956	June 30, 1958
P.L. 85-471, 72 Stat. 241, June 28, 1958	June 30, 1960
P.L. 86-560, 74 Stat. 282, June 30, 1960	June 30, 1962
P.L. 87-505, 76 Stat. 112, June 28, 1962	June 30, 1964
P.L. 88-343, 78 Stat. 235, June 30, 1964	June 30, 1966
P.L. 89-482, 80 Stat. 235, June 30, 1966	June 30, 1968
P.L. 90-370, 82 Stat. 279, July 1, 1968	June 30, 1970
P.L. 91-300, 84 Stat. 367, June 30, 1970	July 30, 1970
P.L. 91-371, 84 Stat. 694, August 1, 1970	August 15, 1970
P.L. 91-379, 84 Stat. 796, August 15, 1970	June 30, 1972
P.L. 92-325, 86 Stat. 390, June 30, 1972	June 30, 1974
P.L. 93-323, 88 Stat. 280, June 30, 1974	July 30, 1974
P.L. 93-367, 88 Stat. 419 , August 7, 1974	September 30, 1974
P.L. 93-426, 88 Stat. 1166, September 30, 1974	June 30, 1975
P.L. 94-42, 89 Stat. 232, June 28, 1975	September 30, 1975
P.L. 94-100, 89 Stat. 483, October 1, 1975	November 30, 1975
P.L. 94-152, 89 Stat. 810, December 16, 1975	September 30, 1977
P.L. 95-37, 91 Stat. 178, June 1, 1977	September 30, 1979
P.L. 96-77, 93 Stat. 588, September 29, 1979	January 28, 1980
P.L. 96-188, 94 Stat. 3, January 28, 1980	March 28, 1980
P.L. 96-225, 94 Stat. 310, April 3, 1980	May 27, 1980
P.L. 96-250, 94 Stat. 371, May 26, 1980	August 27, 1980
P.L. 96-294, 94 Stat. 611, June 30, 1980	September 30, 1981
P.L. 97-47, 95 Stat. 954, September 30, 1981	September 30, 1982
P.L. 97-336, 96 Stat. 1630, October 15, 1982	March 31, 1983
P.L. 98-12, 97 Stat. 53, March 29, 1983	September 30, 1983
P.L. 98-181, 97 Stat. 1267, November 30, 1983	March 30, 1984
P.L. 98-265, 98 Stat. 149, April 17, 1984	September 30, 1986

Public Law and Statutes at Large Citation, and Date of Approval	General Expiration Date[a]
P.L. 99-441, 100 Stat. 1117, October 3, 1986	September 30, 1989
P.L. 101-137, 103 Stat. 824, November 3, 1989	August 10, 1990
P.L. 101-351, 104 Stat. 404, August 9, 1990	September 30, 1990
P.L. 101-407, 104 Stat. 882, October 4, 1990	October 5, 1990
P.L. 101-411, 104 Stat. 893, October 6, 1990	October 20, 1990
P.L. 102-99, 105 Stat. 487, August 17, 1991	September 30, 1991[c]
P.L. 102-193, 105 Stat. 1593, December 6, 1991	March 1, 1992
P.L. 102-558, 106 Stat. 4198, October 28, 1992	September 30, 1995
P.L. 104-64, 109 Stat. 689, December 18, 1995	September 30, 1998
P.L. 105-261, 112 Stat. 2137, October 17, 1998	September 30, 1999
P.L. 106-65, 113 Stat. 769, October 5, 1999	September 30, 2000
P.L. 106-363, 114 Stat. 1407, October 27, 2000	September 30, 2001
P.L. 107-47, 115 Stat. 260, October 5, 2001	September 30, 2003
P.L. 108-195, 117 Stat. 2892, December 17, 2003	September 30, 2008
P.L. 110-367, 122 Stat. 4026, October 8, 2008	September 30, 2009
P.L. 111-67, 123 Stat. 2006, September 30, 2009	September 30, 2014

Source: CRS.

Notes: This table does not include all laws that amended the DPA, only those that altered the termination date of the act, currently codified at 50 U.S.C Appx. §2166, Section 717 of the DPA.

a. Not all provisions of the DPA may have expired on each given date, as the law has frequently offered an evolving set of exceptions to the termination of DPA authorities. For example, as discussed in the "Reauthorization of the DPA" section of this report, currently the majority of DPA authorities will terminate on September 30, 2014, with the exception of four sections.

b. P.L. 83-95 permitted the termination of Titles 2 and 6 as of June 30, 1953, and Titles IV and V to terminate as of April 30, 1953.

c. The termination of authorization from October 20, 1990, to August 17, 1991, is the longest period on record since inception. However, in Section 7 of P.L. 102-99, Congress set the effective date of the passage to October 20, 1990, thus technically authorizing the DPA through this time period.

Author Contact Information

Jared T. Brown
Analyst in Emergency Management and Homeland Security Policy
jbrown@crs.loc.gov, 7-4918

Daniel H. Else
Specialist in National Defense
delse@crs.loc.gov, 7-4996

www.ingramcontent.com/pod-product-compliance
Lightning Source LLC
Chambersburg PA
CBHW080631290526
45790CB00007B/3010